THE WORKSHOP
BOOK OF KNITTING

THE WORKSHOP BOOK OF KNITTING

Ursula von Wartburg

ATHENEUM *1973* NEW YORK

To the children of the Workshop

Acknowledgments

I would like to thank Devereux P. Wight for his constant help and encouragement. I would also like to thank Dieter Luft, William F. Pons, and Gene Bourne for their photographic contributions. The majority of drawings were done by Margrit Senn.

My appreciation goes out to my editor Jean Karl, whose enthusiasm and acceptance made this book possible.

Introduction

The Workshop Book of Knitting was inspired by the children in the workshop that I conduct in New York City. The children attend the workshop for a two hour session once a week during the academic year.

The instructions contained in this book were constantly tested out with the children. Changes were made to insure clarity. If you are a beginner I suggest that you start with the first project. The projects gradually become more involved as you progress. New knitting processes are explained at the end of each project.

The students responded to colors and different kind of materials with great enthusiasm. It is my hope that you will find the joy they had when knitting for yourself or for others.

Contents

THE WORKSHOP
BOOK OF KNITTING

Grazing sheep in the Swiss mountains

Materials and Tools for Knitting

Spinning wool by hand in southern Switzerland

Wool

Wool comes from the soft, curly hair that covers the bodies of sheep. It is sheared during the spring because in summer the animal is more comfortable without its bushy coat of hair. In the fall the hair will have grown back to keep the sheep's body warm for winter.

The hair that has been cut off is brushed and combed to remove leaves and twigs. Then it is washed. The pieces of hair are spun (twisted together) into one long thread called yarn. This process is usually done by machine; but in some places it is still done by hand on a spinning wheel. Hand-spun yarn has a quality all its own. It is uneven and bumpy in spots, which gives it a unique charm not found in machine-made yarn.

Wool knitting yarn is available in hundreds of colors and shades, and in different thicknesses, twists, and textures.

Claudia L., age 14

3

Different Kinds

FIBER	ORIGIN	CHARACTERISTICS
Wool	Fleece of sheep	Soft, resilient, warm.
Mohair	Hair of goats	Soft, lightweight, warm. Because mohair sheds, it is not recommended for baby clothing.
Angora	Hair of Angora rabbits	Fluffy, soft, warm. Sheds. Expensive.
Cotton	Cotton plant	Strong and durable. Absorbent. Not warm.
Linen	Flax plant	Strong and durable. Often mixed with cotton or silk. Has an attractive shine.
Nylon and Orlon	Chemical industry	Wears long, dries fast. Not as warm or absorbent as wool. Often combined with cotton or wool.

of Yarn

Wash gently by hand in luke-
warm water with mild soap. Rinse
in cold water. Do not wring. For
colored materials, add 2 tablespoons
of white vinegar to the final rinse.
Roll in a towel to remove excess water.
Place on a flat surface to dry,
shaping to proper size.

Machine-washable. Can withstand
strong soaps.

Carefully hand-launder or, better
yet, dry-clean.

Machine-washable. Turn garment
inside out before washing. Pat
sweaters into shape on a flat
surface and leave to dry.

Cotton

Cotton comes from a plant grown in
the southern part of the United States
and in other comparable areas of the
world. In April or May the seeds are
planted in rows in huge fields. They
grow into upright plants from 1 to 7
feet tall and branch out in all directions.

Cotton flower

The flowering season of the cotton
plant is during the summer. Only one
or two white flowers open each day,
starting at the bottom of the plant and
up to the top. The flowers wither after
24 hours, turning pink, then blue and
finally purple as they dry and fall off
the plant. The fluffy cotton fiber starts
to grow inside a protective cover called
the *boll*. It takes until fall for the

5

cotton to mature. Then the boll pops open and exposes the fluffy, soft cotton, looking like snowballs and covering the field.

Cotton boll

Cotton is harvested by hand or machine, closely packed into large packages called *bales* and sold to textile mills. There the seeds and twigs are cleaned out, and the cotton is washed and spun into threads. The threads are used for weaving fabrics, knitting, crocheting, and many other purposes.

Cotton yarns are available in many colors and in a wide range of weights and textures. There are thin yarns for crocheting lace around handkerchiefs and embroidering, thick ones for potholders, strong ones for making canvas, and cord, and many other types.

How Yarn Is Sold

Knitting yarn is usually sold in skeins, which are held together by a paper band. Save this band to be sure of getting the same yarn if you have to buy more; it contains important information such as:

Brand name
Amount of yarn in ounces
Thickness
Color name and dye-lot number
Fiber content
Washing instructions

Most skeins are ready for knitting. Look for the beginning of the yarn, which will be inside of the skein. Some skeins, however, are not of the pull-out type and must be rewound into a ball before knitting.

The Basic Weights of Yarn and the Needles to Use

KIND	THICKNESS	NEEDLE SIZE	USES
Baby yarn	Very thin	1–2	Baby clothes and any fine, light, and delicate knitting.
Sport yarn	Thin	2–3	Socks, light pullovers, toys, children's clothing.
Worsted	Medium thick	4–6	Ski wear, blankets, toys, headbands, coat-hanger covers, needle book cover, etc. *Good yarn for beginners.*
Colossal	Extra thick	10	Heavy blankets, house slippers, ski hat, etc.
Rug yarn	Extra thick	9	Potholders, bath mats, shoulder bags, etc.

If you have a tendency
to knit tightly use
the next larger size needle
than the one recommended
and vice versa.

Suggestion: Just for fun, try knitting with unusual materials. For example you might want to show someone at school how to knit by using pencils for needles and shoestring for yarn. Out in the country find two smooth sticks and experiment knitting with tall grasses and hay. For summer project try to knit a hammock with clothesline.

Catherine S., age 12

Winding Yarn

When winding is necessary,

1 Remove the paper band that holds the skein together.

2 Carefully unfold the skein and place it over the back of a chair, or have someone hold it for you. If the skein is divided in half, separate the 2 parts and wind them one at a time.

3 Cut the thin string that is tied around the yarn strands. Look for the yarn ends, which are knotted together around the skein. Cut open close to the knot. Use either end for the beginning.

4 To make sure you won't lose the wrapper that held the skein together, fold the wrapper and wind the yarn around it to form a ball.

Fannie I., age 8

Suggestion: Make a Surprise Ball for someone. Wind candies and little trinkets into a knitting ball. The knitter will be delighted when the surprises fall out as the ball of yarn unwinds. (I remember with pleasure one my grandmother gave me when I was a child. As I knitted, much to my surprise, little notes to me fell out of the ball, and at the end there was a little silver charm.)

Katherine M., age 13

Knitting Needles

Knitting needles are made of either plastic or aluminum. The 2 basic types are single- and double-pointed and they come in a variety of thicknesses and several lengths.

Single-pointed needles are sold in pairs. They have a knob at one end and come in 3 lengths—short (10 inches), medium (12 inches), and long (14 inches).

Double-pointed needles come in sets of 4 or 5 and are usually 7 inches long.

Needle sizes in the United States go from 0 to 14, 0 being the thinnest. In Canada and England it is the reverse, with 0 being the thickest.

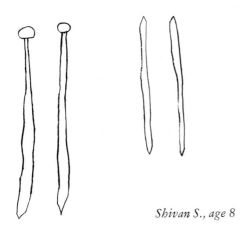

Shivan S., age 8

Other Helpful Tools

Scissors for cutting yarn, paper, and cardboard.

Ruler for measuring knitting and paper.

Pencil. Besides writing with it, you will use it in making a twisted cord.

Notebook for keeping knitting patterns, designs, and ideas; also for sketching projects.

Paper clip. Hang a paper clip onto the knitting yarn and slide it next to the last knitted stitch as a marker.

Tapestry needles, sizes 18 and 20, for sewing together knitted pieces and sewing in yarn ends. It is easy to thread these needles because they have large eyes. They also have dull points.

Crochet hook, which is a straight needle with a hook at one end, for crocheting and for picking up dropped stitches. Use size F for medium-thick yarn and size 2 for thin yarn.

Safety pins, small and medium sizes, for weaving drawstrings into knitting.

Handkerchief, man's size, for wrapping delicate knitting.

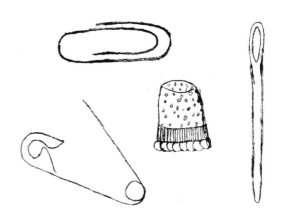

Claudia L., age 14

Cable needle for holding stitches when knitting cable patterns. (You can also use a wooden match or any short double-pointed needle for a cable needle.)

Stitch holder, which looks like a large safety pin, for holding stitches. (You can also thread stitches onto a piece of yarn to hold them.)

Row knitting

What You Need to Know

Row Knitting

Two needles are used in row knitting. You hold the needle with the work on it in your left hand and knit the work off onto the empty needle in your right hand. When you have knitted all the stitches from one needle onto the other you have knitted 1 row. To continue knitting, go back and forth, turning the work around at the end of each row.

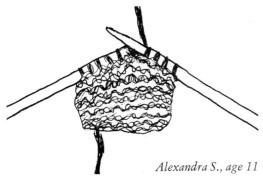

Alexandra S., age 11

Make it a habit to finish the row before putting aside your knitting. But, if you had to put down your knitting before finishing the row, make sure you pick it up again the right way. The needle holding the last knitted stitch goes in your right hand.

The Plain Stitch

Catherine S., age 12

The plain stitch is the basic stitch in knitting. You see plain stitches all over the stockinette pattern. Most often pullovers and feet of socks are knitted in this pattern. The plain stitch has a flat, even surface. If you inspect a single stitch you will find it looks like the letter V. The reverse side of a plain stitch is bumpy and is called a purl stitch (see page 12).

Electra R., age 10

The Purl Stitch

The second most important stitch is the purl stitch. You can see it on the inside of your socks' feet. It is almost never used alone as a pattern stitch; but combined with the plain stitch it forms interesting patterns. The reverse side of a purl stitch is a plain stitch (see page 11).

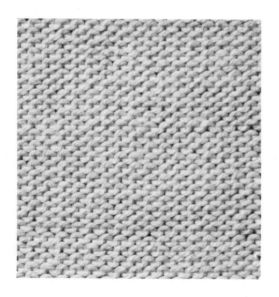

The Garter Row Pattern

The garter row pattern consists of ridges that run across the knitting parallel to the needle. The ridges are purl stitches and the valleys in between are plain stitches. The ridges come about because the rows of plain stitches on the inside are rows of purl stitches on the outside. The pattern looks the same on both sides.

KNITTING INSTRUCTIONS

To knit garter rows you only have to know how to do the plain stitch, and then knit it continuously on both sides of your work. By plain-knitting 2 rows, you make 1 garter row.

Always count garter rows on the outside of the knitting.

How to Tell the Outside from the Inside

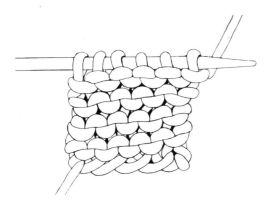

The outside of the knitting is the side you will want to show.

When you cast on stitches, a piece of the measured length of yarn is left over. If this leftover piece is on your left, you are looking at the outside of the knitting. If the piece of yarn is on your right, you are looking at the inside of the knitting.

You can also tell the difference between outside and inside by the casting-on edge. The inside of the casting-on edge is bumpy compared with the outside.

Inside

Outside

How to Take Care of Your Knitting

1 Store your knitting tools and materials in a box such as a shoe box, and keep light-colored knitting wrapped up in a handkerchief or dishtowel.

2 Don't let the ball of wool roll around on the floor while you are knitting.

3 Wash your hands with soap and water before starting to knit. Also wash them if they become moist and sticky while knitting.

4 Do not rest your elbows on a table while knitting. Sit back in your chair and relax.

5 Make it a habit to finish the row or round before putting your knitting away.

Catherine S., age 12

6 When you put your knitting away, place one needle over the other and wrap yarn around the needles so the stitches won't slide off.

7 Make your workplace a happy place to be. Tidy up around you. Work with good light on your knitting.

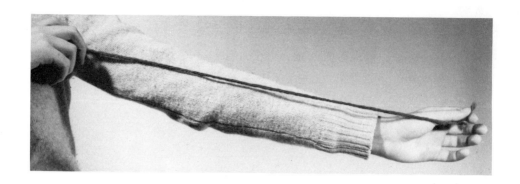

How to Make a Slipknot

It is important to know how to make a slipknot because it is the basis of knitting. The first stitch you put on the needle *is* a slipknot, and the following stitches are similar to it although made a little differently.

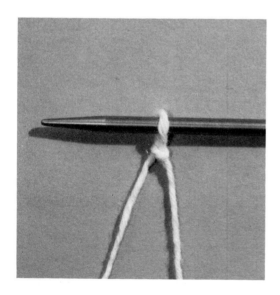

1 Cut a piece of yarn about 2 arms' length and straighten it out in front of you on a table.

2 Make a small loop in the yarn by crossing one side over the other.

3 Take the piece of yarn that crosses in front and bring it under and across the back of the loop.

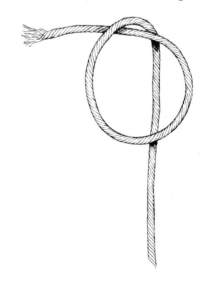

4 Pull through the loop the part of the yarn that is crossing in back, while lightly holding both strands with the other hand. Tighten the slipknot.

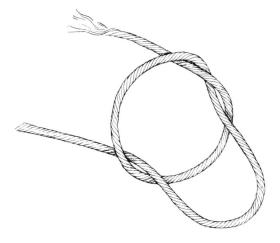

5 Pull each yarn end to see which one makes the loop smaller. Pull on the loop if you want to make it bigger.

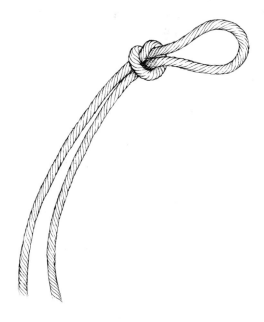

Suggestion: To practice making slip-knots, make them an inch or so apart. Place candies, flowers or small bundles of different-colored yarn strands in the loops and make a necklace or bracelet. Use a longer piece of yarn if you want to make a belt or headband.

Casting On for Beginners

To start your knitting you must know how to cast on stitches. In this process you make slipknots out of 2 strands of yarn and place them on a knitting needle.

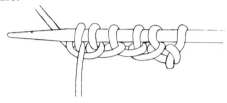

1 Find the beginning of the yarn (see page 6). Make a slipknot (see page 14) 1 arm's length from the beginning. Do not cut the yarn.

2 Put the slipknot onto a knitting needle and tighten it loosely around the needle. This is your first stitch. Hold the needle in your right hand like holding a handle.

3 About ½ inch from the first stitch make a small loop in the measured length of yarn *with the free end crossing over in front*. Hold the loop in your left hand.

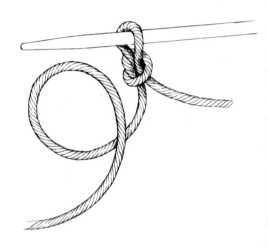

4 Bring the yarn coming from the ball across the back of the loop.

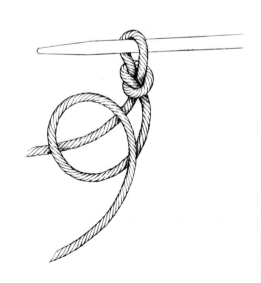

5 Pass the needle, top to bottom, under the yarn that crosses in back of the loop. Pull the yarn up through the loop and onto the needle. This is the second stitch.

6 Tighten the second stitch by pulling on both strands under the needle.

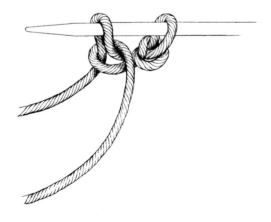

7 Repeat steps 3 through 6 for as many stitches as you need to cast on.

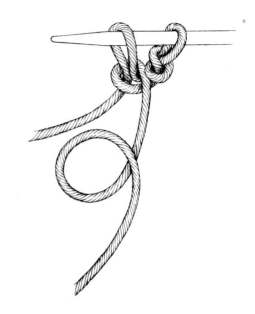

8 Cut the measured piece of yarn, leaving about 3 inches.

Casting On a Faster Way

Rule: 1 needle's length of yarn makes about 10 stitches. Add an extra needle's length for good measure.

1 Measure out the needed length of yarn and make a slipknot at that point. Put the slipknot on the needle 1 inch from the tip and tighten it loosely around the needle.

17

2 Now place your right hand over the needle with your thumb on the stitch and hold the needle in your hand the way you would hold a handle.

3 Hold the 2 yarn strands in your left hand, with the last 3 fingers closing over them.

4 Push the strands apart with your left index finger and thumb, the measured strand against your thumb. Spread the 2 fingers as far apart as you can.

5 Bring the needle over to the thumb so that the yarn crosses and makes a loop.

6 Bring the tip of the needle up through the loop on your thumb.

7 With the tip of the needle catch the other strand and pull it through the loop.

Important: Be sure you don't tighten the stitches too much; they must slide easily on the needle. If your stitches keep coming out too tight, try casting on over 2 needles and then pulling one needle out.

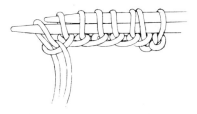

8 Pull your thumb out of the loop and put it under the needle, behind the measured strand. Now swing your thumb out against the strand, tightening the stitch. At the same time you will be forming a new loop around your thumb.

9 Repeat steps 5 through 8 for the number of stitches you need.

Project 1

Knitting a Bookmark

and Learning How to Do the Plain Stitch

Knitted by Janine A., age 12

MATERIAL NEEDED

Small amount of medium-thick yarn
1 pair of short knitting needles, size 4

WORK METHOD

Casting on
Row knitting
Binding off (see page 24).

PATTERN STITCH

Garter rows (see page 12).

KNITTING INSTRUCTIONS

1 Cast on 6 stitches.

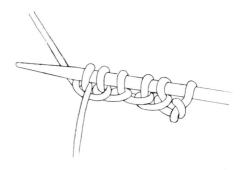

2 Get ready to knit:
   a Hold the needle with the cast-on stitches in your right hand, the way you would hold a handle.
   b Spread apart the fingers of your left hand and loosely wind the yarn from the ball over your little finger, in across the middle and ring fingers, then out and twice around the index finger.

c Practice pulling the yarn through your fingers. If the yarn does not slide easily, wash your hands with soap and water. Try again.

d Switch the needle over into your left hand. Hold it near the tip with your last 3 fingers and thumb closed over the stitches.

e Check the position of each finger. *Index finger* is up. Its job is to hold the yarn. *Middle finger* and *thumb* must hold the stitch that is nearest to the tip of the needle. This keeps it from slipping off. *Ring finger* and *little finger* help to hold the needle.

f The empty needle is held near the tip with all fingers of the right hand, as you would hold a handle.

3 Learning how to do the plain stitch

a Put the tip of the right-hand needle between the first 2 stitches and up through the bottom of the first stitch, front to back.

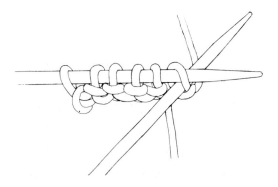

b Pass the needle over the strand of yarn coming from your left index finger. Bring the needle around the yarn. Hold the yarn with your index finger so it won't slip off.

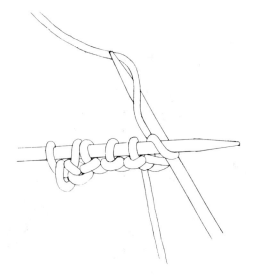

c Bring the needle with the yarn on it back through the stitch.

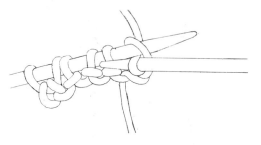

d Slide off the stitch on the left-hand needle and tighten the new stitch on the right-hand needle.

e Repeat steps a through d to the end of the row.

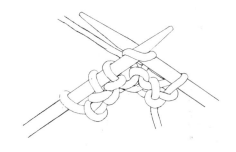

It helps to count rhythmically 1-2-3-4 as you do each step, or to say to yourself at each step:

a through the stitch
b yarn around
c bring yarn back
d slide off old stitch

4 How to switch needles to start a new row:

a Bring the yarn coming from the left index finger under the needle, then switch the needle, with the tip away from you, over into your left hand again. Make sure the yarn is under and behind the needle.

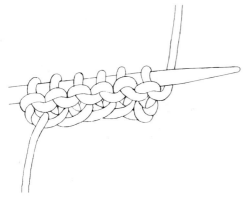

b Take the empty needle in your right hand.

5 Plain-knit the second row. Knit slowly and carefully.

6 Plain-knit until you have 5 garter rows (or 10 rows of plain-knitting). Compare your work with the photograph.

7 Bind off. (See page 24.)

FINISHING INSTRUCTIONS
Sew in yarn ends.

How to Bind Off

This is a way of finishing off knitting. It makes a firm edge that won't unravel. As a rule bind off in your pattern stitch and on the outside of the knitting.

KNITTING INSTRUCTIONS

Be sure to knit each stitch loosely.

1 Plain-knit the first 2 stitches.

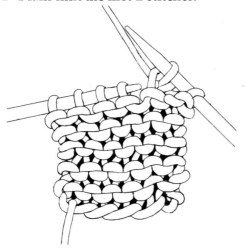

2 With the point of the left-hand needle loosen the back stitch, then pull the front stitch through it and let the back stitch go.

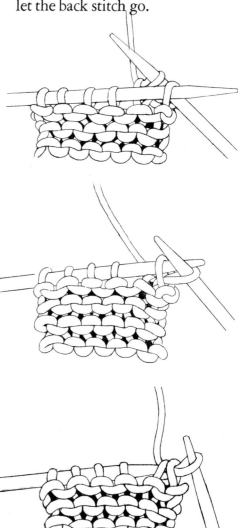

3 Plain-knit another stitch onto the right-hand needle.

4 Again loosen the back stitch and pull the front stitch through it, letting the back stitch go (as in step 2).

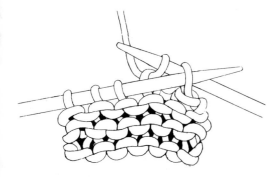

5 Repeat steps 3 and 4 to end of row. You will have 1 stitch left over at the end.

6 Cut the yarn about 3 inches from the stitch. Bring the yarn up through the stitch. Remove the needle and pull the stitch tight.

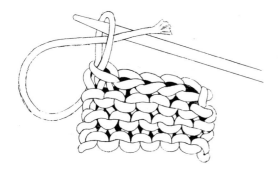

Project 2

Headband

You can knit a headband in a few hours. Make a narrow one for school on 6 stitches and a wide one to keep your ears warm for winter on 16 stitches.

Knitted by Katie D., age 9

MATERIAL NEEDED

1 small skein of knitting worsted
1 pair of short knitting needles, size 4
(See page 8.)
1 tapestry needle

WORK METHOD

Casting on
Row knitting
Knotted edge (See page 28.)
Binding off

PATTERN STITCH

Garter rows

KNITTING INSTRUCTIONS

* This symbol means make a knotted edge. See page 28 for instructions.

1 Cast on 6 stitches.

2 Plain-knit all 6 stitches on the first row.

3 *Plain-knit until you have 3 garter rows. Be sure you always have 6 stitches on the needle.

4 Compare your knitting with the photograph. If it looks the same, continue; if not, rip out the knitting and start over. Plain-knit carefully to avoid making the following mistakes:

a dropping a stitch;

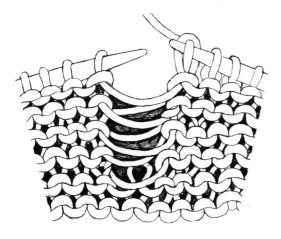

b forgetting to bring the needle with the yarn on it back through the stitch;

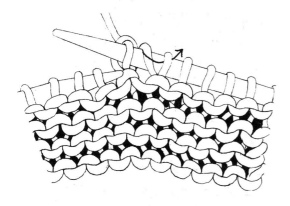

c splitting the yarn of the stitch with the point of the needle;

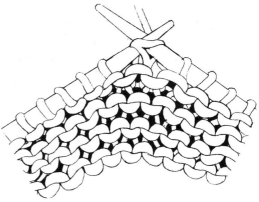

d inserting the right-hand needle through the row below instead of through the stitch on the needle;

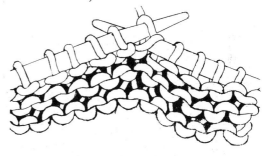

5 *Plain-knit until you have a total of 36 garter rows.

6 Stretch the knitting lightly and try it around your head. If necessary plain-knit a few more rows.

7 *Bind off on the outside of the knitting. Leave 1 arm's length of yarn for sewing the headband together.

FINISHING INSTRUCTIONS

1 Sew the casting-on and binding-off edges together.

2 Sew in any yarn ends along the knotted edge.

27

The Knotted Edge

A knotted edge is firm and has a finished look. It is used in row knitting and is made with the first and last stitches of every row. If you find it difficult to make the knotted edge on the first row after casting on, however, it is all right to plain-knit the very first stitch.

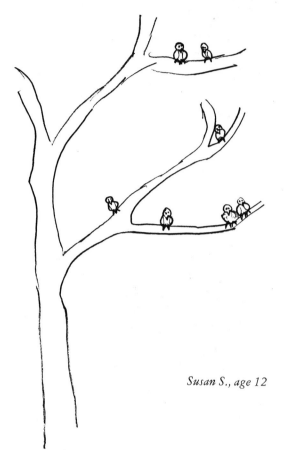

Susan S., age 12

KNITTING INSTRUCTIONS

*Slip the first stitch on the row over to the empty needle without knitting it. Plain-knit the last stitch on the row.

The symbol *, is used throughout the knitting instructions in this book to remind you to make a knotted edge. Whenever you see the symbol *, before a step in the instructions, *slip the first stitch and plain-knit the last stitch on the row.*

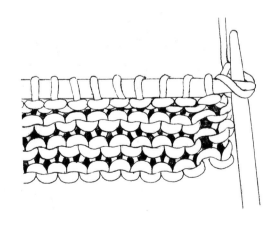

28

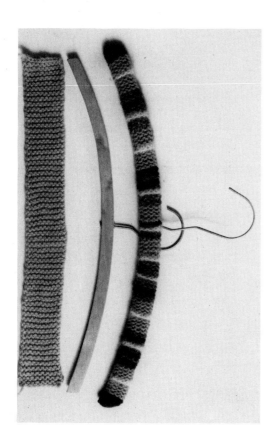

Hanger Cover

Another good project for practicing the plain stitch is this cover for a wooden hanger. Knit covers in solid colors or in stripes. They make practical gifts and usually sell well at a bazaar.

MATERIAL NEEDED

1 small skein of knitting worsted or small amounts of leftover yarn in several colors for a striped cover
1 pair of short knitting needles, size 4 (See page 8.)
1 straight wooden hanger
1 tapestry needle

WORK METHOD

Casting on
Row knitting
Knotted edge
Binding off
Joining yarn to change colors if this will be a striped cover

PATTERN STITCH

Garter rows

Margot O., age 12

29

KNITTING INSTRUCTIONS

*Knotted edge

1 Cast on 10 stitches.
2 Plain-knit all 10 stitches on the first row.
3 *Plain-knit until you have 8 garter rows. Compare your knitting with the photograph. At this point tie a marker of different colored wool around the knitting yarn and slide it next to the last knitted stitch.
4 *Plain-knit until you have about 45 garter rows. Be sure you always have 10 stitches on the needle. Try to avoid mistakes.
5 Stretch your knitting lightly and hold it along the hanger to check the length. If necessary plain-knit more rows to fit. See photograph. Finish knitting on an inside row.
6 *Bind off. Leave 3 arms' lengths of yarn for sewing.

FINISHING INSTRUCTIONS

1 Fold the casting-on and binding-off edges in half and sew each edge together on the outside of the knitting.
2 If you knitted a striped cover, end off each colored strand through knitting of the same color.
3 Count the total number of garter rows and find the center. Push the hanger hook through the center.
4 Pull the ends over the hanger and sew together the knotted edges at the bottom of the hanger.

How to Join Yarn and Change Colors

Join yarn to continue knitting when you come to the end of a ball or skein, or to create patterns with various colors and textures of yarn. There is no limit to the color combinations and special effects. Collect leftover yarn and either sketch your color arrangement or create a design as you knit. (See the sketches by Katherine M., age 10.)

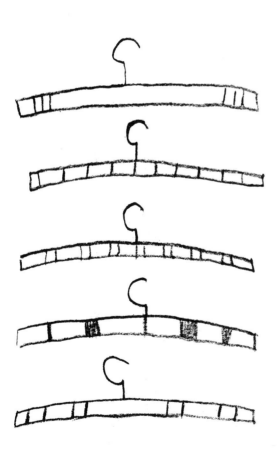

KNITTING INSTRUCTIONS
Row Knitting

1 Knit to the last stitch on the inside row.

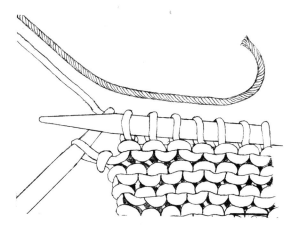

2 Put the new yarn alongside the old one and plain-knit the last stitch with both yarns. Drop the old yarn and cut it about 4 inches from the stitch.

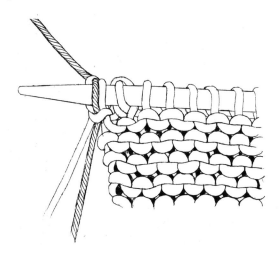

3 Put the new yarn on your hand and continue to knit.

Treat the 2-yarn stitch as a single stitch. Make sure to start each new color at the same edge.

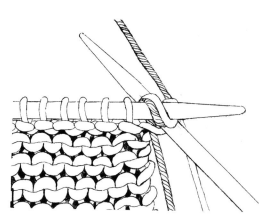

Note: When changing colors in a scarf knitted in the garter-row pattern, plain-knit 1 stitch, purl 1 stitch on the first row with each new color. This keeps the knitting looking the same on both sides.

Round Knitting

1 Knit to the end of a round.

2 Tie the new and the old yarns together loosely right next to the last knitted stitch. The free ends of yarn must be at least 3 inches long.

3 Keep the knot on the inside of the knitting and continue knitting with the new yarn.

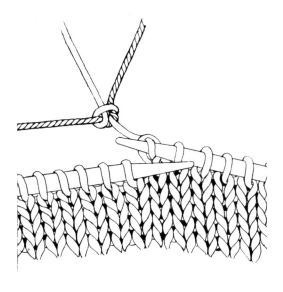

4 The knot will be undone and the ends sewn in when you are finishing the project. (See page 140.)

How to Use a Marker

A marker marks a specific place in your knitting. From that point, it is easy to count stitches or rows. A marker also lets you see immediately where you started increasing or decreasing, for instance, and can be most helpful in knitting complicated patterns such as cabling, where you have to repeat a certain process every so many rows.

A marker can be:

1 A piece of contrasting-colored yarn either sewn into the knitting or tied around the knitting yarn and then moved next to the last knitted stitch.

2 A paper clip or bobby pin.

How to Correct a Mistake

There are several ways to correct a mistake in your knitting. Choosing the right method depends on the pattern stitch and the location of the mistake.

ON THE NEEDLE

When there is a mistake in the row you are knitting on, you can take out or "undo" as many stitches as necessary without pulling out the needles. The work is held the same way it is when you are knitting.

1 Insert the tip of the left needle through the front of the stitch below the last knitted one on the right-hand needle.

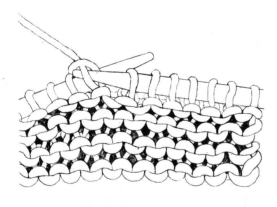

2 Slip the stitch off the right needle and pull the yarn to undo it.
3 Repeat steps 1 and 2 until you have undone all the stitches you want; then reknit the stitches.

IN THE KNITTING

1 For stockinette and ribbing patterns:

  a Knit to the stitch directly above the mistake.

  b Drop the stitch off the needle and undo it row by row until you get down to the mistake. This will form a "ladder," like a run in a stocking.

  c With a crochet hook loop each rung of the ladder through the stitch below, moving from the bottom up. When the stitch is worked all the way back up to the needle, be sure to place it on the needle, facing in the same direction as the other stitches.

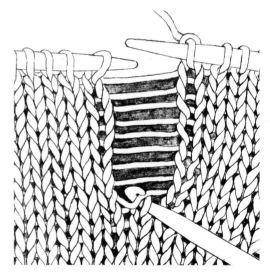

Note: Plain-knit stitches are easier to pick up than purl stitches. To pick up purl stitches, turn the knitting around and do it from the other side.

2 For garter rows and complicated patterns:

   a Pull the needles out of the knitting.

   b Pull on the yarn to unravel as much of the knitting as necessary, stopping at the end of a row.

   c Hold the knitting in your left hand the way you would if you were knitting.

   d Take the needle in your right hand and insert the point, back to front, through the stitch that is right under a loose stitch.

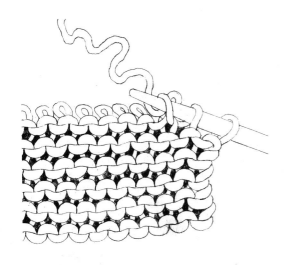

   e Pull the yarn just enough to undo that loose stitch. Undoing this extra row helps you to get all the stitches correctly back onto the needle.

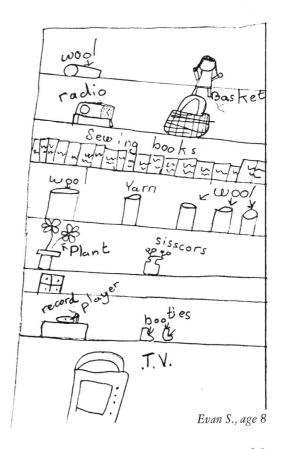

Evan S., age 8

35

Project 4

Needle Book

This is a most useful little project. The cover is knitted; the pages are made of felt. Keep your tapestry needles on one page, safety pins on another, then fine sewing needles and pins. Paper clips for knitting markers can be hooked on the inside of the cover. A needle book is handy when traveling. It makes a nice gift.

KNITTING INSTRUCTIONS

*Knotted edge

A Knitting the cover from side to side:

1 Cast on 20 stitches.
2 *Plain-knit 34 garter rows.
3 *Bind off.

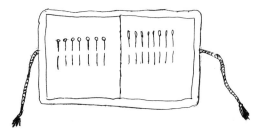

Julie B., age 11

MATERIAL NEEDED

1 small skein of knitting worsted or small amounts of leftover yarn in several colors
1 pair of short knitting needles, size 4 (See page 18.)
1 tapestry needle

WORK METHOD

Casting on
Row knitting
Knotted edge
Binding off
Joining yarn to change colors (optional)

PATTERN STITCH

Garter rows

Knitted by Julie B., age 11

B Knitting the cover from bottom to top:
1 Cast on 31 stitches.
2 *Plain-knit 19 or 20 garter rows.
3 *Bind off.

FINISHING INSTRUCTIONS

1 Sew in all yarn ends on the inside. If you changed colors sew through knitting of the same color.

2 Cut 6 pieces of yarn each one arm's length.

3 Sew 3 pieces together through the center of the edge of the front and back covers. See illustration.

4 Bring the ends together and braid the three doubled strands. Tie knots at the ends.

5 Cut 2 double pages of felt slightly smaller than the cover.

6 Place the felt pieces against the inside of the cover.

7 Sew the pages to the cover.

Knitted by Jennifer M., age 10

Project 5

Indoor Ball

This is an ideal ball for playing with in the house. It is soft, lightweight, has a nice bounce and is almost noiseless. Wash it in warm water and mild soap, and rinse well. The ball takes a few days to dry.

MATERIAL NEEDED

2 ounces of knitting worsted or small amounts of leftover yarn in several colors
1 pair of short knitting needles, size 4 (See page 8.)
Stuffing material (See page 54.)
1 tapestry needle

WORK METHOD

Casting on
Row knitting
Knotted edge
Joining yarns to change colors (optional)
Binding off

PATTERN STITCH

Garter rows

MAKING THE INSIDE OF THE BALL

1 Cut a rag or torn nylon stockings into pieces.

2 Bunch the pieces into a ball and, if available, put a layer of synthetic fiber stuffing all around it.

3 Wind yarn around the ball to hold it together. See illustration. Ball has to be firm and well shaped.

Knitted by Caroline F., age 9

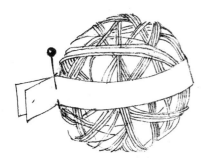

FINDING OUT HOW MANY STITCHES TO CAST ON

1 Measure the ball by putting a strip of paper around it tightly.

2 Half of this measurement is the casting-on width. You will knit a strip long enough to fit around the ball.

KNITTING THE COVER
*Knotted edge

1 Cast on stitches equal the width. Spread apart the cast-on stitches on the needle. See illustration.

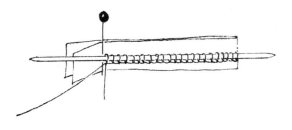

2 *Plain-knit as many garter rows as needed to fit the knitting tightly around the ball.

3 *Bind off. Leave 1 arm's length of yarn for sewing.

FINISHING INSTRUCTIONS

1 Sew casting-on and binding-off edges together to form a ring.

2 With tapestry needle, draw a piece of yarn through the knotted edge on one side.

3 Pull together the opening. Bring the yarn through the knots once more, pulling the opening completely closed.

4 Fold all yarn ends inside and place the ball in the cover.

5 Sew and pull together the other opening as in steps 2 and 3.

Knitted by Joan G., age 14

Project 6

Scarf

This different-looking scarf is fun to knit and takes surprisingly little time because of the extra-long stitches. To make the long stitches, you will be using a ruler or strip of cardboard in place of a needle. You can vary the number of garter rows.

MATERIAL NEEDED

6 ounces of knitting worsted
1 pair of knitting needles, size 8 (extra large)
1 12-inch ruler about 1 inch wide, or a strip of cardboard about the same shape.

WORK METHOD

Casting on
Row knitting
Knotted edge
Binding off

PATTERN STITCH

Garter rows

KNITTING INSTRUCTIONS

*Knotted edge

1 Cast on 36 stitches.

2 *Plain-knit until you have 10 garter rows.

3 Slip the first stitch, pull it up, and put it onto a ruler. See illustration. Plain-knit each stitch and slip it onto the ruler for the entire row.

4 Knit the stitches off the ruler onto
the needle. Pull on the needle after
each stitch to keep the stitches the
size of the ruler.

Knitted by Beatrice R., age 12

5 Count the stitches on the needle.
There should be 36.

6*Plain-knit 10 garter rows.

7 Repeat steps 3 through 5 until your
scarf is as long as you want. End
with 10 garter rows.

8*Bind off. Leave a half arm's length
of yarn.

FINISHING INSTRUCTIONS

1 Sew in all yarn ends.

2 Add fringe. (See page 44).

Knitted by Soledad A., age 9

Beatrice

Scarf

1st cast on 36

two different colors

3 means 3 garter rows and 2
means 2
garter rows

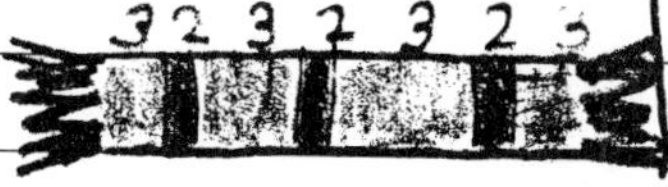

3 2 3 2 3 2 3

red + light purple

After I finished the scarf,
I gave it to our nurse
for Christmas. She
wears it all the time
so I guess she really
likes it.

A page from Beatrice R.'s notebook

Fringe

Add fringe to scarves and belts. Sew fringe to a doll's head and it becomes hair. A bunch of fringe is a horse's tail. Decorate the edges of a purse with fringe. For an unusual effect make long fringe and knot beads among the strands.

Alexandra D., age 15

INSTRUCTIONS

1 Cut pieces of yarn twice the desired length of the fringe.

2 Fold each piece of yarn in half and thread both ends through a large tapestry needle.

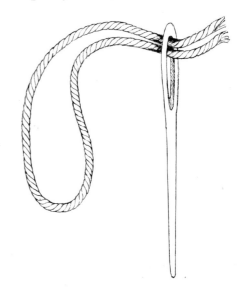

44

3 Pull the needle through the first cast-on stitch on the edge of a scarf, for example. Watch for the loop; don't pull it all the way through the stitch.

4 Draw the needle through the loop. Pull on both strands to tighten the loop.

5 On the binding-off side, fringe is put through the chain stitches. Elsewhere fringe can be put on as desired.

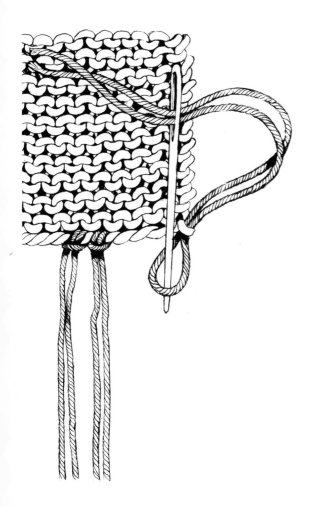

Project 7

Twisted Cord

Twisted cords can be made thick or thin, single or multicolored and have as many different textures as there are kinds of yarn to twist. Use twisted cords for drawstrings in bags, ties on baby clothes, belts, hair ribbons, etc. While learning how to twist yarn into cord, make yourself a few hair ribbons.

Hair ribbons made by Katie D., age 9

MATERIAL NEEDED

Large amount of medium-thick yarn
1 doorknob
1 pencil
1 pair of scissors

INSTRUCTIONS

1 Measure out a piece of yarn the length of a hair ribbon (try it around your head) and then cut a length of yarn 6 times that length.

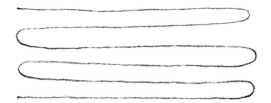

2 Straighten out the cut piece of yarn and fold it in half. Hook the fold on a doorknob and pull back both ends; tie a knot.

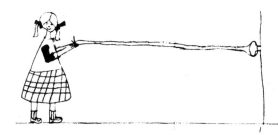

3 Put a pencil between the strands and slide it up against the knot. Pull the yarn tight, away from the door-knob.

4 Hold the yarn very close to the pencil with one hand. With the index finger of the other hand turn the pencil like a propeller. Stop when the yarn is twisted all the way to the doorknob.

Drawings by Caroline F., age 9

5 Now lay a pair of scissors across the twisted yarn. Have someone hold the scissors while you fold the yarn over them and bring the end with the pencil to the doorknob. *Keep the yarn stretched tight at all times.*

6 Take the yarn off the doorknob and loop it around the pencil, keeping the twisted yarn taut.

7 Without slackening the yarn, hold the pencil up high and let the scissors dangle freely. You may have to stand on a chair so the scissors don't touch the floor. Let the scissors spin around. Stop them as soon as they start turning in the opposite direction.

8 Slip the yarn off the pencil and *quickly*, before the cord has a chance to untwist, tie a knot 1 inch from the end. Remove the scissors and tie a knot at that end. Cut the yarn on the outside of each knot to form 2 little tassels.

Note: If you want to make a thicker cord use 2 or more strands of yarn. The finished cord looks pretty if the strands are different colors. If you use very thick rug yarn measure out 8 to 10 times the length of the finished twisted cord.

Project 8

Puff Balls

Puff balls are fun to make. In various sizes and colors, they look adorable hanging in a bunch from the top of a baby's crib. Sew them to the ends of a tie string, on top of a ski hat, to ice-skate laces. Attach a tiny one to a zipper pull, key chain, or electric-light pull.

Puff ball made by Tina A., age 14

MATERIAL NEEDED

Large amount of any yarn
1 cup or glass
1 small thread spool
1 pair of scissors
Thin cardboard
1 large tapestry needle
1 pencil

INSTRUCTIONS

1 Holding a cup upside down near the edge of a piece of thin cardboard, make 2 circles by tracing around the cup.

2 Cut out the circles with scissors.

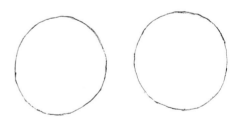

3 Place a small thread spool in the center of each circle and trace around it.

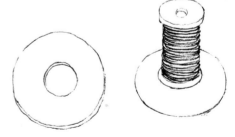

4 Cut out the inside circles, making 2 rings. Place 1 ring on top of the other.

48

5 Cut a piece of yarn 10 arms' length long. Fold it in half and wind it evenly around the 2 rings together, covering the entire surface of the rings. See illustration. Continue winding, pulling the yarn up through the hole, over the ring, and up through the hole again, until the hole is almost filled, using a tapestry needle to get the yarn through the hole as it fills up. You may want to use various colors of yarn.

6 Now slip one blade of a scissors down through the yarn and between the 2 cardboard rings and cut the yarn around the outer edge.

7 Cut 1 arm's length of yarn. Wind it tightly a few times around the middle between the 2 rings and tie a knot. Thread the yarn ends into the tapestry needle and draw them through the center to the other side. Tie the ends together for hanging the ball, for sewing it to a hat, tie string, etc.

Project 9

Chickadee

You can't imagine how lovable these birds are until you have felt how soft and fluffy they are. You might want to make a whole flock.

Buttercup is the name of my chick. She's all different shades of yellow but she has an orange beak and tiny green eyes. I cuddle with her at nighttime because she's so fluffy and soft. She likes to get under my covers and keep warm. It may sound silly that she's cold at night with all of that fur but she's only a chick.

Britt B., age 9

8 Pull out the cardboard rings. Fluff up the ball by hitting it sharply against the edge of a table.

9 Trim the ball to a nicely rounded shape.

chickadee

MATERIAL NEEDED

Large amount of any yarn

Cardboard for rings

1 small thread spool

Felt for beak

Orange or white pipe cleaners for legs and feet

Black wool for eyes

1 tapestry needle

INSTRUCTIONS

Maro C., age 10

1 Make 2 puff balls, one teacup-size and one eggcup-size (see page 48); *but do not remove cardboard rings.*

2 Spread apart the 2 cardboard rings of each ball and sew the balls together closely at their centers.

3 Pull out the cardboard rings. Fluff up the balls and trim them to the shape of a chicken.

4 Cut a beak out of felt. Fold it in half and sew it with fine thread to the center of the head.

5 Sew a piece of medium-thick black yarn through the head for eyes.

6 Fold a pipe cleaner in half and bend the ends to suggest feet. With fine thread sew the pipe cleaner to the bottom of the body.

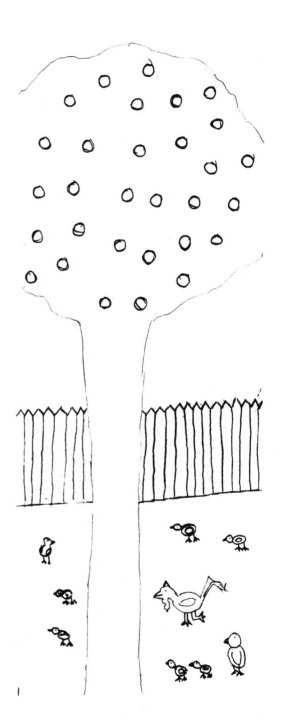

Project 10

Mother Cat
and Kitten

Claudia L., age 14

These soft, cuddly cats are loved by children of all ages. Knit a whole family with each kitty a different color, or knit tigers instead, with brown and yellow stripes. Here you will do the purl stitch for the first time.

WORK METHOD

Casting on
Row knitting
Knotted edge
Joining yarn to change colors if knitting tigers
Binding off

MATERIAL NEEDED

1 small skein of knitting worsted or some leftover yarn in several colors.
1 pair of short knitting needles, size 4 (See page 8.)
Stuffing material (See page 57.)
1 tapestry needle
1 small piece of ribbon

PATTERN STITCH

Garter rows
Purling (See page 55.)

Knitted by Pamela E., Margot O., Julie B., Valerie D.

KNITTING INSTRUCTIONS

*Knotted edge

Front and back are knitted as one piece, then folded at the top of the head.

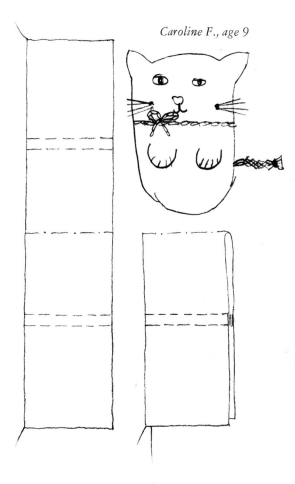

Caroline F., age 9

Mother Cat

1 Cast on 16 stitches.

2 Plain-knit all 16 stitches on the first row.

3 *Plain-knit until you have 13 garter rows. Finish knitting on an inside row.

4 *Plain-knit 1 row. ⎫
  *Purl 1 row. ⎭ neck front

5 *Plain-knit 22 garter rows. Finish on an inside row.

6 *Plain-knit 1 row. ⎫
  *Purl 1 row. ⎭ neck back

7 *Plain-knit 13 garter rows. Finish on an inside row.

8 *Bind off. Leave 1 arm's length of yarn for sewing.

FINISHING INSTRUCTIONS

1 Fold the knitting in half and sew together as shown in illustration.

2 Stuff and then sew the bottom together.

3 Tie a ribbon around the neck.

4 Indicate ears with running stitches across the corners.

5 Embroider the face.

6 Make a tail:

   a Cut 3 pieces of yarn, each 1 arm's length.

   b Sew the three pieces to the back near the bottom.

   c Bring all the ends together and braid the three doubled strands. Tie a knot at the end.

Knitted by Valerie D., age 8

Kitten

1 Cast on 8 stitches.

2 Plain-knit all 8 stitches on the first row.

3 *Plain-knit until you have 7 garter rows. Finish on an inside row.

4 *Plain-knit 1 row. } neck front
  *Purl 1 row.

5 *Plain-knit 10 garter rows. Finish on an inside row.

6 *Plain-knit 1 row. } neck back
  *Purl 1 row.

7 *Plain-knit 7 garter rows. Finish on an inside row.

8 *Bind off. Leave 1 arm's length of yarn for sewing.

Materials for Stuffing

Many of the projects in this book call for stuffing material. To have stuffing when you need it, start collecting suitable material now in a special bag or box. Among the materials to collect are:

Absorbent cotton
Nylon stockings, cut into small pieces
Fabric, cut into small pieces
Bits and pieces of yarn
Unraveled yarn from old socks and pullovers

You can also stuff with hay and, of course, upholstery stuffing, which you can buy.

Note: Avoid shredded foam rubber, which is hard and bumpy.

Alexandra D., age 15

How to Do the
Purl Stitch

(It's like making a plain stitch backward.)

1 Bring the yarn in front of the left-hand needle, beside the stitch.

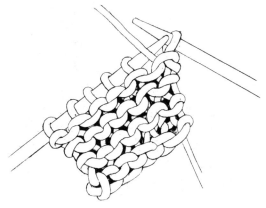

2 Put the tip of the right-hand needle under the yarn and through the stitch from back to front.

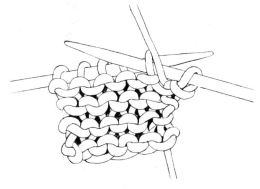

3 Pass the needle over the strand coming from the right index finger. Bring the needle around the yarn. Hold the yarn with your left thumb so it won't slide off the needle.

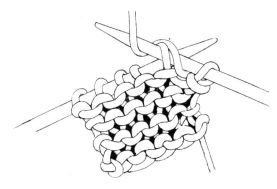

4 Bring the needle with the yarn on it back through the stitch.

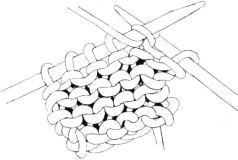

5 Slide off the stitch on the left-hand needle and tighten the stitch on the right-hand needle.

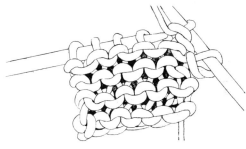

6 Repeat steps 1 through 5 to the end of row.

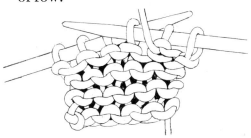

The Stockinette Pattern

The stockinette pattern is the smoothest, most even knitting pattern. The outside shows nothing but plain stitches, while the inside is all purl stitches. It is frequently used for pullovers and mittens and is what you almost always see on the feet of stockings. The plain stitches in stockinette are easy to follow when embroidering or mending worn places.

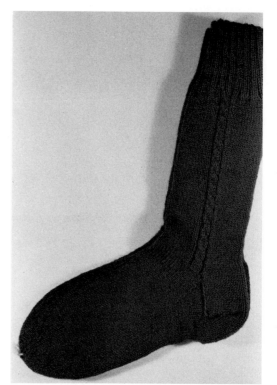

Knitted by Diana H., age 14

KNITTING INSTRUCTIONS

Row Knitting. Plain-knit all outside rows and purl all inside rows.

Round Knitting. Plain-knit continuously for the same result.

You can count rows and rounds on either side, but it is easier to count them on the inside.

Project 11

Teddy Bear

This teddy bear is about 7 inches tall. To make one twice as tall, double the number of stitches and rows in the instructions. By using thicker or thinner yarn and needles, you can also change the size.

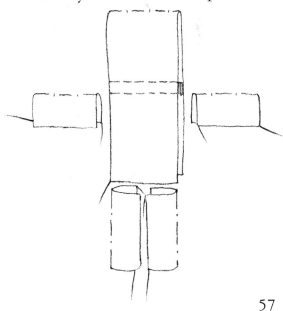

Big bear knitted by Electra R., age 10

Small bears knitted by Serena R. and Alexandra S., age 12

Janine A., age 12

MATERIAL NEEDED

2 ounces of knitting worsted
1 pair of short knitting needles, size 4
(See page 8.)
Stuffing material
1 tapestry needle

WORK METHOD

Casting on
Row knitting
Knotted edge
Binding off

PATTERN STITCH

Garter rows
Purling

The teddy bear is knitted in 5 parts.

KNITTING INSTRUCTIONS

*Knotted edge

Arm (make 2)

1 Cast on 12 stitches.
2 *Plain-knit until you have 12 garter rows.
3 *Bind off. Leave 1 arm's length of yarn for sewing.

Body and Head

1 Cast on 12 stitches.
2 *Plain-knit until you have 12 garter rows.
3 *Plain-knit 1 row.
  *Purl 1 row. } neck front
4 *Plain-knit 20 garter rows.
5 *Plain-knit 1 row.
  *Purl 1 row. } neck back
6 *Plain-knit 12 garter rows.
7 *Bind off. Leave 1 arm's length of yarn for sewing.

Leg (make 2)

1 Cast on 12 stitches.
2 *Plain-knit until you have 12 garter rows.
3 *Bind off. Leave 1 arm's length of yarn for sewing.

FINISHING INSTRUCTIONS

1 Fold and sew together 2 sides on each piece.
2 Stuff each part and sew the opening together.
3 Sew the arms and legs to the body.
4 Indicate ears with running stitches across the corners as shown.
5 Embroider the face.

Caroline F., age 8

58

Project 12

Horse

The size of this horse depends partly on the thickness of the wool and needles. The small one was knitted on size 2 needles with baby yarn and half the number of stitches and rows given in the instructions below.

WORK METHOD

Casting on
Row knitting
Knotted edge
Casting *in* stitches. (See page 63.)
Binding off.

PATTERN STITCH

Garter rows

MATERIAL NEEDED

Any kind of yarn
1 pair of short knitting needles, the size depends on the thickness of yarn. (See page 7.)
Stuffing material
1 tapestry needle
Felt or leather scraps for ears

Knitted by Margot O., age 12

KNITTING INSTRUCTIONS

*Knotted edge

The horse is knitted as one piece. The same 2 needles are used throughout this project.

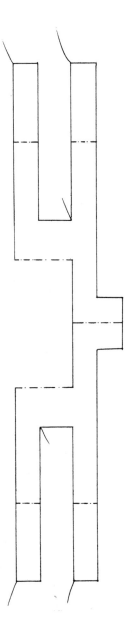

First Leg

1 Cast on 6 stitches.

2 *Plain-knit until you have 32 garter rows.

3 *Do not bind off; but cut the yarn leaving about 4 inches.

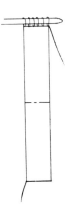

Second Leg

1 Cast on 6 stitches onto the empty needle.

2 *Using both needles, plain-knit the second leg until you have 32 garter rows. Do not cut the yarn. (Both legs should be on one needle.)

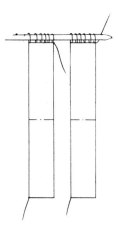

Body

1 *Plain-knit the 6 stitches over the first leg on the needle, cast *in* 8 stitches (see page 63), plain-knit the 6 stitches over the second leg. (You should now have 20 stitches on the needle.)

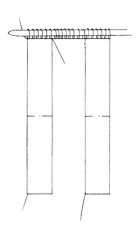

2 *Plain-knit until you have 8 garter rows over the 20 stitches.

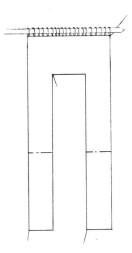

Neck

*Plain-knit 8 garter rows over the first 6 stitches on the needle only, leaving the other stitches on the needle, but not knitting them.

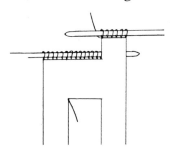

Head

1 Cast *in* 6 stitches.

2 *Plain-knit 11 garter rows over the 12 stitches.

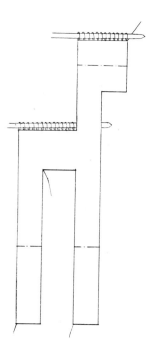

Neck

1 *Bind off 6 stitches, then plain-knit the 5 stitches remaining on the left-hand needle.

2 *Plain-knit 8 garter rows over the 6 stitches.

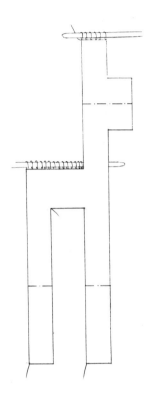

Body

1 *Plain-knit across the neck; then plain-knit the 14 stitches that you are holding on the left-hand needle to finish the row.

2 *Plain-knit 8 garter rows over the 20 stitches.

3 *Plain-knit the first 6 stitches, then bind off 8 stitches and plain-knit the

5 stitches remaining on the left-hand needle for the third leg. (You have 12 stitches on the needle with a gap in between.

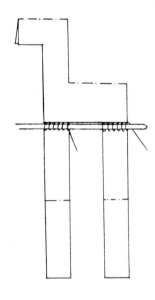

Third Leg

1 *Plain-knit over the 6 stitches on the needle until you have 32 garter rows.

2 *Bind off. Leave 1 arm's length of yarn for sewing.

Fourth Leg

1 *With the yarn from the ball, plain-knit over the 6 stitches on the needle as before, until you have 32 garter rows.

2 *Bind off. Leave 1 arm's length of yarn for sewing.

FINISHING INSTRUCTIONS

1 Fold the legs in half and sew up the sides, stuffing as you go.

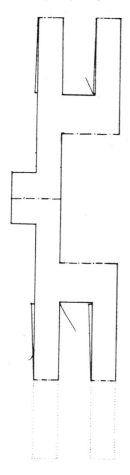

2 Fold the knitting in half with the open ends of the legs together. Sew the horse together, stuffing as you go.

3 Make a mane and a tail. (See page 44 for fringe.)

4 Embroider eyes and a mouth.

5 Sew on ears cut out of felt or leather.

How to Cast *in* Stitches

Casting *in* is a way to bring in new stitches after you have started to knit. It is usually done at the end of a row to extend the width.

KNITTING INSTRUCTIONS

1 Make a small loop, the yarn from the ball crossing in front.

2 Put the needle through the loop, front to back, and tighten the stitch. See drawing.

3 Repeat steps 1 and 2 for the required number of stitches.

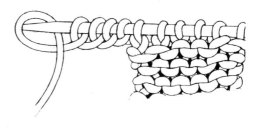

Project 13

Drawstring Bag

You can knit a drawstring bag in cotton or wool and in various sizes to hold all kinds of things. Use bags to hold change, eyeglasses, marbles, a compact, or school supplies. Make one of cotton twine and fill it with bits of soap for a sudsy scrubber to use in the shower. Fill another with pine needles or lavender blossoms and hang it in the linen closet.

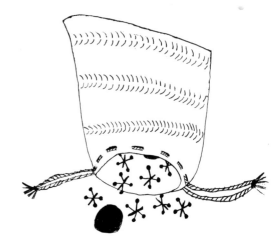

Fannie I, age 8

Knitted by Serena R., age 11

KNITTING INSTRUCTIONS

Work out your own knitting instructions. Make your knitting twice the length that the bag will be, then fold it in half. Knit a knotted edge. (For finishing, see page 140.) Make drawstrings of twisted cords (project 7) and weave them in and out between stitches with a small safety pin. You might want to make a paper pattern to help in deciding on size, color scheme, and pattern stitch for your bag. To know how many stitches to cast on you might want to make a knitting gauge.

How to Gauge Knitting

A knitting gauge is a sample of the pattern stitch knitted with the yarn you plan to use on 10 to 20 stitches. With it you can gauge *width* to know how many stitches to cast on and *length* for the number of rows to knit. If you find you are knitting 5 stitches to an inch, for example, you must cast on 25 stitches for a width of 5 inches.

Blocking

Blocking means to form the knitting into its final shape on a flat surface and to flatten down the stitches for an even, smooth appearance.

FOR BLOCKING BY HAND

1 Wash the knitting and pat it into shape on a towel on a flat surface.

2 Let dry.

FOR BLOCKING BY STEAM

Always block the pieces of a garment before sewing them together.

1 Turn knitting inside out and lay it on an ironing board.

2 Pat into proper shape. Compare measurements with knitting instructions. Stretch lightly if necessary. Pin at corners and edges into the board to hold in shape.

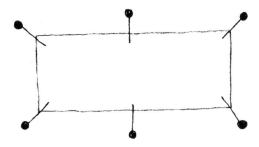

3 Then either:

  a Gently iron with a steam iron. Pat to smooth down stitches. Or:

  b Cover knitting with a damp cloth (dishtowel). Without pressing down, move a hot iron over the damp cloth to produce steam.

Laura B., age 11

Warning: Never steam garter rows or ribbing. Doing so spoils the elastic quality. Do not press down on the iron. Never touch knitting directly with a hot iron.

Project 14

Doll's Bed

In this project you will again work out your own knitting instructions. The knitted pieces are small, so feel free to experiment, even at the risk of having to do something over.

MATERIAL NEEDED

Small amounts of knitting worsted and fine sport yarn or baby yarn

2 pairs of knitting needles, sizes 2 and 4. (See page 7.)

A large kitchen matchbox or other box about 2 inches x 3 ½ inches

1 handkerchief or piece of white cloth for pillowcase and sheets (optional)

Stuffing material

1 tapestry needle

WORK METHOD

Casting on

Row knitting

Knotted edge

Joining yarn to change colors (optional)

Binding off

PATTERN STITCH

Garter rows

Stockinette

KNITTING INSTRUCTIONS
You will be making the following:

1 mattress of knitting worsted
1 blanket of knitting worsted
1 pillow of baby yarn or sport yarn
1 or 2 sheets of baby yarn or sport yarn
or use a small white handkerchief for a sheet.

1 Make 2 gauges each 10 stitches wide to use for measuring. Make one of knitting worsted with size 4 needles and another of baby yarn or sport yarn with size 2 needles.

2 Use your gauges to find out how many stitches to cast on for each piece of knitting. (See page 65.) Make the mattress the width of the bed, and the pillow a little narrower. You may or may not want the blanket and sheet to tuck in.

3 Mattress and pillow are knitted double length, then folded in half, sewn, and lightly stuffed.

4 Finish off each piece with care.

Much joy!

Project 15

Baby Doll

This doll is small enough to fit nicely into the little doll's bed. (See page 66.)

MATERIAL NEEDED

A small quantity of baby yarn or sport yarn
1 pair of short knitting needles, size 2
1 piece of nylon stocking (for head)
Stuffing material
Fur for the hair, or make it of yarn fringe
Glue
1 tapestry needle

WORK METHOD

Row knitting
Knotted edge
Binding off

PATTERN STITCH

Garter rows
Stockinette

KNITTING INSTRUCTIONS

*Knotted edge

Front

1 Cast on 26 stitches.

2 *Plain-knit 2 rows.

3 Slip the first stitch, plain-knit 7 stitches, purl 10 stitches, plain-knit 8 stitches.

4 *Plain-knit 1 row.

5 Repeat steps 3 and 4 once.

6 Again slip the first stitch, plain-knit 7 stitches, purl 10 stitches, plain-knit 8 stitches.

7 *Bind off 8 stitches, then plain-knit the 17 stitches remaining on the left-hand needle.

8 *Bind off 8 stitches, plain-knit the 9 stitches remaining on the left-hand needle.

9 *Plain-knit 12 garter rows.

10 *Bind off. Leave 1 arm's length of yarn for sewing.

68

Back

1 Cast on 26 stitches.

2 *Plain-knit until you have 4 garter rows.

3 *Bind off 8 stitches, plain-knit the 17 stitches remaining on the left-hand needle.

4 *Bind off 8 stitches, then plain-knit the 9 stitches remaining on the left-hand needle.

5 *Plain-knit until you have 17 garter rows, counting from the casting-on edge.

6 *Bind off. Leave 1 arm's length of yarn for sewing.

FINISHING INSTRUCTIONS

1 Sew the front and back together. Leave open at the top.

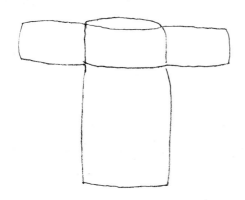

2 Stuff the arms lightly.

3 For the head, form a ball of stuffing and stretch the piece of nylon stocking around it. Tie it together securely with a piece of yarn. See illustration.

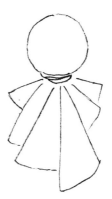

4 Place the head between the shoulders and sew the edges together, so that the head is held in place.

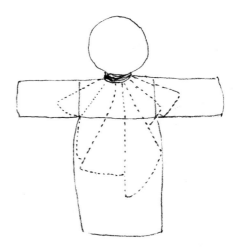

5 Sew in all yarn ends.

6 For hair, glue a bit of fur to the head, or use yarn fringe.

7 Embroider a face if you wish, or leave it to your imagination.

Project 16

Baby Bootees: 1 to 3 Months

Make these bootees and give them to a mother for her baby. Instead of binding off to finish this knitting, you will end by knitting together stitches at the toe of the bootee.

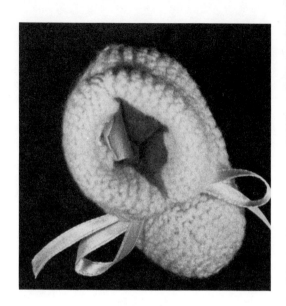

Make 2 bootees. Right and left are the same. The bootee is folded in half at the bottom of the foot.

MATERIAL NEEDED

2 ounces of baby yarn
1 pair of short knitting needles, size 2. (See page 8.)
1 yard of silk ribbon or handmade cord. (See page 46 for twisted cord.)
1 tapestry needle
1 small safety pin

WORK METHOD

Casting on
Row knitting
Knotted edge
Binding off
Ending off by decreasing. (See page 72.)

PATTERN STITCH

Garter rows

Knitted by Wendy B., age 13

KNITTING INSTRUCTIONS

*Knotted edge

1 Cast on 58 stitches.

2 *Plain-knit until you have 15 garter rows or 2¼ inches. Finish on an inside row.

3 *Bind off 12 stitches. Plain-knit the 45 stitches remaining on the left-hand needle.

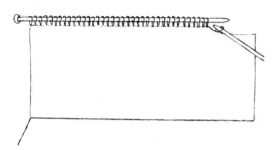

4 *Bind off 12 stitches. Plain-knit the 33 stitches remaining on the left-hand needle. (You should have 34 stitches on the row.)

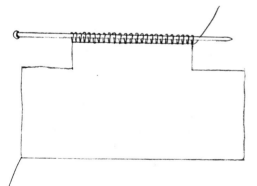

5 *Knit 9 garter rows (24 counting from the casting-on edge, or 3½ inches).

6 Ending off by decreasing

a *Plain-knit together 2 stitches. Repeat to end of row. (You should have 18 stitches left on the row.)

b *Plain-knit 1 row.

c *Plain-knit together 2 stitches. Repeat to end of row. (You should have 10 stitches left on the needle.)

d *Plain-knit 1 row.

7 Cut the yarn leaving 1 arm's length for sewing. Using a tapestry needle draw the yarn through the 10 stitches on the needle. See illustration. Remove the knitting needle. Draw the yarn through again in the same direction and pull the stitches together tightly.

FINISHING INSTRUCTIONS

1 Fold the knitting in half and sew the bootee together.

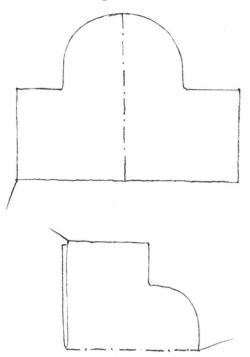

2 Attach the ribbon or cord to a safety pin. Weave it over and under 2 garter rows all around the bootee. See photograph. Cut the ends at a 45-degree angle to keep the fabric from fraying.

Knitted by Janine A., age 12, using medium thick wool and the same number of stitches.

Ending Off by Decreasing

You usually end off row knitting by binding off. Another way is to decrease the number of stitches rapidly until there are only a few left. Those last few stitches are then strung onto the yarn end and gathered together tightly. This makes a slightly rounded ending.

KNITTING INSTRUCTIONS

1 Plain-knit or purl together 2 stitches. Repeat to end of row.

2 Knit 1 row in your pattern stitch.

3 Repeat steps 1 and 2.

4 Cut the yarn and string the stitches remaining onto it.

Katri B. with her little brother.

Project 17

Slippers

These warm, comfortable slippers make good presents because they stretch to fit almost any foot. You may also want to sew a cotton bag to carry them in when traveling.

Jennifer M., age 10

MATERIAL NEEDED

4 balls (8 ounces) of knitting worsted
1 pair of short knitting needles, size 8
1 large tapestry needle

WORK METHOD

Row knitting
Knotted edge
Ending off by decreasing

PATTERN STITCH

Garter rows
Ribbing (See page 75).

KNITTING INSTRUCTIONS
*Knotted edge

Knit with double yarn, using the yarn from 2 balls at the same time. This reinforces the slipper for greater strength and longer wear.

1 Cast on 32 stitches.
2 Knit tightly. Plain-knit 10 stitches, then purl 1, plain-knit 10, purl 1, plain-knit 10.
3 *Plain-knit 1 row.
4 Slip the first stitch directly to the right-hand needle, then plain-knit 9, purl 1, plain-knit 10, purl 1, plain-knit 10.
5 *Plain-knit 1 row.
6 *Follow step 4 for all inside rows and plain-knit all outside rows until you have knitted 15 garter rows.
7 *Rib 18 rows: purl 1, plain 1.
8 Ending off by decreasing:
  a *Plain-knit together 2 stitches. Repeat to end of row. (You should now have 17 stitches left on the needle.)
  b *Purl 1 row.
9 Cut the yarn, leaving 1 arm's length. Using a large tapestry needle, draw the yarn through the stitches. Remove the knitting needle. Draw the yarn through

again in the same direction and pull the stitches together tightly.

FINISHING INSTRUCTIONS
1 Fold the knitting in half.
2 Sew together the knitting at the heel and for the length of the ribbing at the toe.
3 Sew in all yarn ends.

Caroline F., age 9, making a twisted cord. See page 46.

The Ribbing Pattern

In the ribbing pattern, ribs or ridges run up and down the knitting at right angles to the needle. Because the pattern is elastic, it is used for borders on sweaters, socks, hats and mittens. As the pattern for an entire garment, ribbing has an interesting texture and is formfitting. The ridges are formed of plain stitches. The valleys are purl stitches.

KNITTING INSTRUCTIONS

The most common ribbing patterns are the following: plain 1 stitch, purl 1 stitch; plain 2, purl 2. See illustration.

The first row is knitted according to the chosen pattern. In all following rows plain stitches are knitted above plain stitches and purl stitches are knitted above purl stitches, to form plain ribs and purl valleys.

Hold the yarn in back to plain-knit, bring it forward to purl.

For a tighter fitting border cast the stitches onto one of the regular needles, then knit them off and rib the border on needles a few sizes thinner. After finishing the border change back to the regular needles.

Knitted by Catherine S., age 12

Project 18
Ski Hat

There is a variety of designs to choose from if you want to embroider your ski hat (See page 78). Or, you might want to make your own pattern on graph paper. You could also design your own hat and then figure out the knitting instructions. Measure tightly around your head with a strip of paper and cast on stitches to fit this measurement. End off your own creation the same way as the ski hat below (steps 6 and 7).

MATERIAL NEEDED

4 ounces of knitting worsted
1 pair of short knitting needles, size 4
(See page 8.)
Contrasting colors of the same kind of yarn for embroidering
1 tapestry needle

WORK METHOD

Casting on
Row knitting
Knotted edge
Ending off by decreasing

PATTERN STITCH

Ribbing
Stockinette

Knitted for her brother by Laura B., age 10

76

KNITTING INSTRUCTIONS

*Knotted edge

You may want to knit the ribbing on smaller needles for a tighter fit. (See page 75.)

1 Cast on 118 stitches.

2 *Rib 3 rows: Plain-knit 2, purl 2.

3 *Stockinette 20 rows or about 2¼ inches by plain-knitting on the outside and purling on the inside.

4 *Rib 23 rows or about 2½ inches. **Finish ribbing on an outside row.**

5 *Stockinette 5 inches **but this time** plain-knit on the **inside** and purl on the **outside.**

6 End off by decreasing:
   a *Plain-knit together 2 stitches, repeat to end of row. (You should have 60 stitches on the needle.)
   b *Purl 1 row.
   c *Plain-knit together 2 stitches. Repeat to end of row. (You should now have 30 stitches.)
   d *Purl 1 row.

7 Cut the yarn, leaving 1 arm's length. Using a tapestry needle, draw the yarn through the stitches. Remove the knitting needle. Draw the yarn through again in the same direction and pull stitches together tightly.

FINISHING INSTRUCTIONS

1 Block the stockinette part of the knitting; **be careful not to steam the ribbing.**

2 Sew the hat together and sew in all yarn ends.

3 Embroider design.

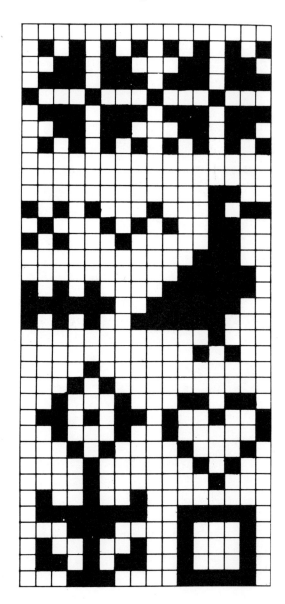

Project 19

Knitting Squares

A knitted square has four sides, which must be equal. There are three ways to knit squares. You can make them any size you want.

You can knit squares out of pieces of leftover yarn. Fine yarn can be used double to match the thickness of heavier yarn. Then the squares can be sewn together to make a poncho, a scarf, a hat. Two squares can be sewn together to make a bag. Knitting a patchwork blanket of squares can become a family project.

Either knit the squares in whatever colors you have and then arrange them in a pattern, or make a color sketch first and carefully follow it.

MATERIAL NEEDED

Odds and ends of yarn
Knitting needles. (See page 7.)

WORK METHOD

Casting on
Row knitting
Knotted edge
Increasing stitches with yarn-overs. (See page 82.)
Increasing by plain-knitting 2 stitches out of 1 stitch. (See page 82.)

Knitted by Swiss children, 7th grade

Decreasing by knitting together stitches. (See page 83.)
Binding off

PATTERN STITCH

For straight method—any pattern stitch
For right-angle method—garter rows
For diagonal method—garter rows

KNITTING INSTRUCTIONS

*Knotted edge
Select one of the following three methods.

Right-Angle Method

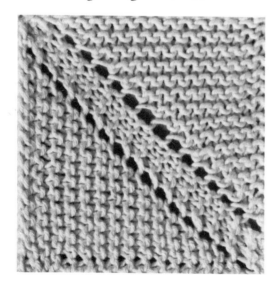

1 Cast on 5 stitches.
2 Plain-knit all stitches on the first row.

3 For the next row slip the first stitch, yarn-over, plain-knit the 3 middle stitches, yarn-over, plain-knit the last stitch.

4 *Plain-knit one row. You should now have 7 stitches on the needle because of the yarn-overs.

5 *Plain-knit to the 3 middle stitches, yarn-over before and after the middle stitches, then plain-knit to the end of the row.

6 *Plain-knit one row. There are now 9 stitches.

7 *Continue as above, alternating between steps 5 and 6, increasing every other row.

8 *Bind off.

Note: To check the size of the square, knit to the center of any row. Place the knitting flat on a table and position the needles at right angles.

Diagonal Method

Straight Method

1 Cast on 3 stitches.

2 Plain-knit all stitches on the first row.

3 On the next row, slip the first stitch, plain-knit to the last stitch, then increase by plain-knitting 2 stitches out of the last stitch. (See page 82.)

4 Repeat step 3 until the knitting has reached the right width.

5*From now on decrease by plain-knitting the last 2 stitches on every row until you have only 3 stitches left on the needle.

6*Bind off.

1 Cast on as many stitches as you need to make the square the size you want.

2*Knit the same number of garter rows as you have stitches on the needle, or until the piece is exactly square. Fold diagonally to test length.

3*Bind off.

Design for poncho by Amy M., age 15

How to Make a Yarn-Over

Plain-Knitting

1 Knit to the place where you want the yarn-over to be. Then bring the yarn to the front and over the right-hand needle, making a loop over the needle. Hold the yarn on the needle and continue to knit.

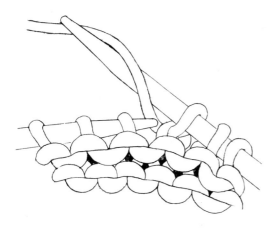

Purling

2 Purl to the place where you want the yarn-over to be. Then again bring the yarn to the front and over the needle and back to the front ready to purl the next stitch.

Different Ways to Increase Stitches

You can increase the width of your knitting these three ways:

1 *Plain-knitting 2 stitches out of 1*
At the place where you want to add a stitch make a plain stitch, but leave the old stitch on the left-hand needle. Plain-knit through it again but at the back of the needle.

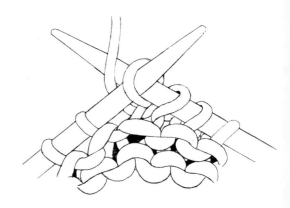

2 *Making a stitch from a yarn-over*
Where you want to add a stitch make a yarn-over. In the following row knit the yarn-over just as you would any other stitch. To avoid leaving a hole you can plain-knit through the back of the yarn-over, which gives it a twist.

3 Adding stitches by casting in

a Make a small loop, the yarn from the ball crossing in front.

b Put the needle through the loop, front to back, and tighten the stitch.

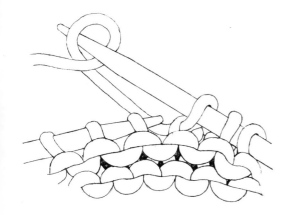

Shivan S., age 8

Different Ways to Decrease Stitches

There are three ways to decrease 1 stitch:

1 *Plain decreasing*—plain-knit together 2 stitches.

2 *Purl decreasing*—purl together 2 stitches.

3 *Slip decreasing*—slip 1 stitch, plain-knit 1 stitch, then pull the slip stitch over the knitted stitch.

There are three ways to decrease 2 stitches:

1 *Double plain decreasing*—plain-knit together 3 stitches.

2 *Double purl decreasing*—purl together 3 stitches.

3 *Double slip decreasing*—slip 1 stitch, plain-knit together 2 stitches, then pull the slip stitch over.

83

Project 20

Baby Bib

This pretty little bib for an infant is made of cotton yarn and is machine-washable. You may want to crochet a border.

MATERIAL NEEDED

1 ball of cotton yarn (such as Knit-Cro-Sheen)
1 pair of short knitting needles, size 2. (See page 8.)
1 tapestry needle

WORK METHOD

Casting on
Row knitting
Knotted edge
Increasing by plain knitting 2 stitches out of 1
Decreasing by plain knitting together stitches

PATTERN STITCH

Garter rows

KNITTING INSTRUCTIONS

*Knotted edge

1 Cast on 3 stitches (bottom corner).

2 Plain-knit all stitches on the first row.

3 Slip the first stitch, plain-knit to the last stitch, then increase by plain-knitting 2 stitches out of the last stitch. (See page 82.)

4 Repeat step 3 until the knitting is from 6½ to 7 inches wide. Finish with an even number.

5 *Plain-knit to the center of the row. Turn the knitting around. (Hold the other half of the stitches on the needle, but do not knit them. From now on you will be knitting each half separately.)

6*Decrease by plain-knitting together the last 2 stitches on every row until there are only 3 stitches left on the needle.

7*Bind off.

8*Plain-knit the second half the same as the first, by starting at the center and following steps 5 and 6.

FINISHING INSTRUCTIONS

1 Sew in all yarn ends.

2 For the tie strings

a Make a slipknot and place it loosely onto a knitting needle.

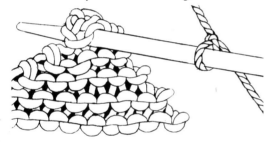

b Poke the needle through one of the top corners, wrap the yarn once around the needle, and bring the needle with the yarn on it back through the same place in the corner.

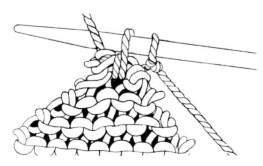

c Wrap the yarn once more around the needle and draw it through the 2 stitches on the needle.

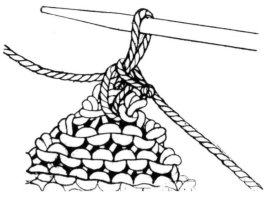

d Finger crochet a tie string about 11 inches long.

e Repeat for other corner.

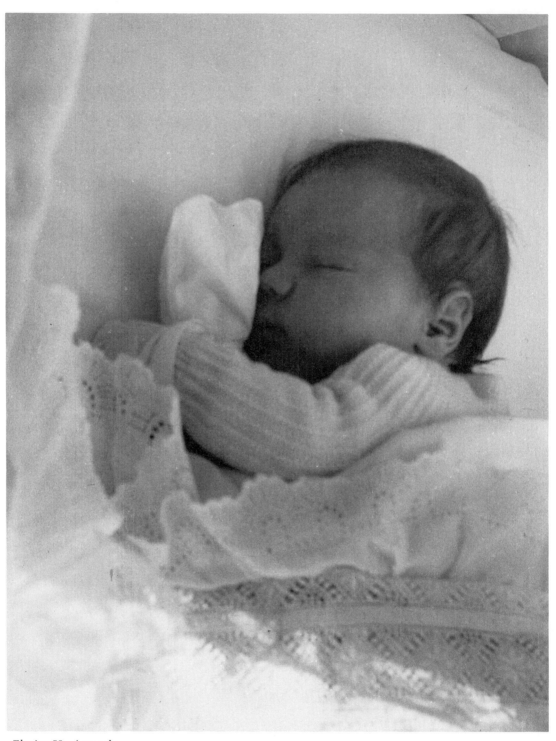

Florian H., 4 months

Designing Patterns with Plain and Purl Stitches

Design your own knitting patterns using these symbols:

| for plain stitch .

— for a purl stitch

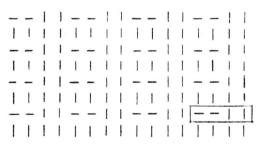

Draw your design on graph paper, using the 2 symbols to represent the stitches as they will appear on the outside of the knitting project. Draw enough of the pattern to visualize what it will look like.

HOW TO USE YOUR KNITTING DIAGRAM

This knitting diagram represents the pattern of the knitting in the photograph. The knitting diagrams in this book only tell you what the knitting will *look* like on the outside. It is up to you to figure out what stitches to knit to get the patterns indicated on the diagrams.

In row knitting be especially careful that your stitches come out the same as on the diagram. (A purl stitch on the inside is a plain stitch on the outside.)

FITTING THE DIAGRAM TO YOUR KNITTING

Count the stitches in one sequence of a row (circled parts of diagrams). The number of stitches you will cast on must be a multiple of the number in one sequence. If necessary, add or subtract a few stitches to make the pattern fit or to make it look the same at both edges. For row knitting, add 2 stitches for the knotted edge.

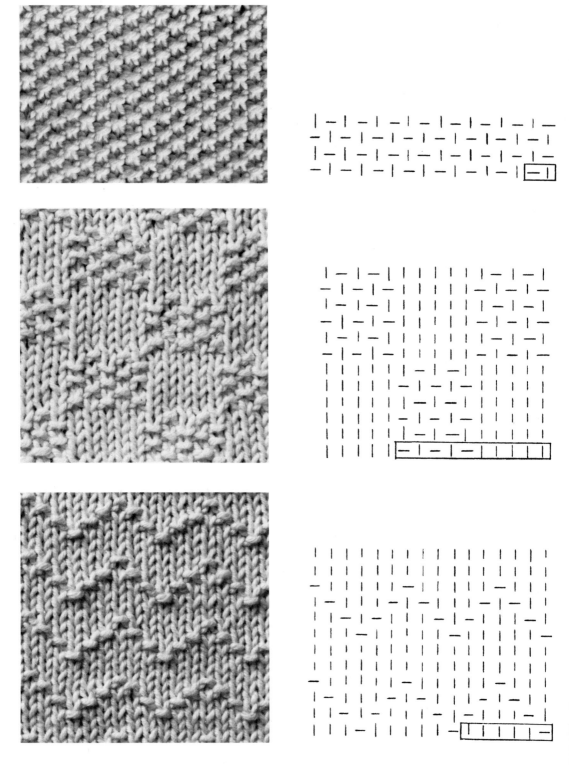

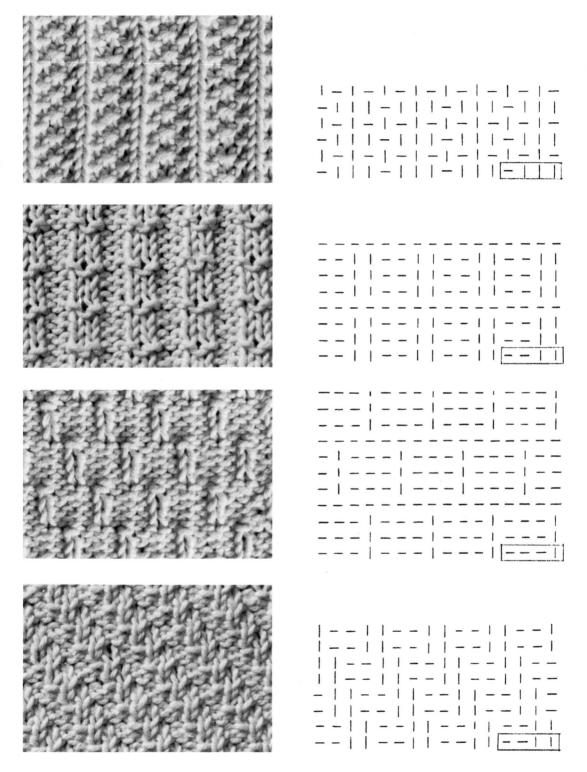

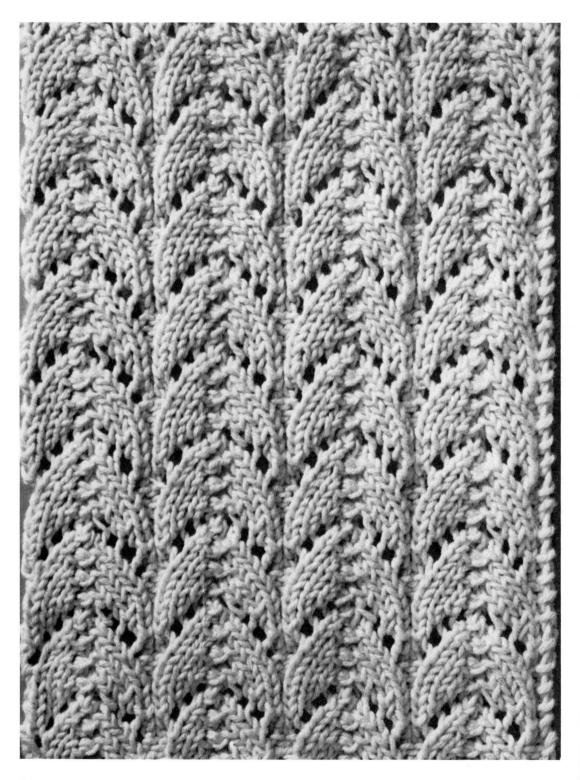

Knitting Lace Patterns

To read the diagrams in this book for lace patterns or to design your own lace patterns, you will need to know the following knitting symbols:

1 | for a plain stitch.

2 — for a purl stitch.

3 ⁄ for 2 plain stitches knitted together.

4 = for 2 purl stitches knitted together.

5 ∧ for a slip decrease stitch.
  (Slip 1 stitch, plain-knit the second stitch, then pass the slip stitch over the knitted stitch.)

6 ∩ for a yarn-over.

7 ⌒ for 2 yarn-overs.
  (Place the yarn over the right-hand needle from front to back twice. In the following row, plain-knit the first yarn, over and purl the second.)

8 ≡ for 3 purl stitches knitted together.

9 ⋏ for a double slip decrease stitch.
  (Slip the first stitch, plain-knit together 2 stitches, then pass the slip stitch over the plain decreasing stitch.)

Note: In the diagrams for lace patterns yarn-overs are always balanced by decreasing to keep the number of stitches on the needle the same.

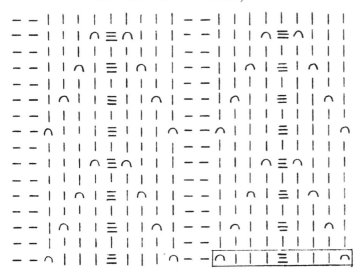

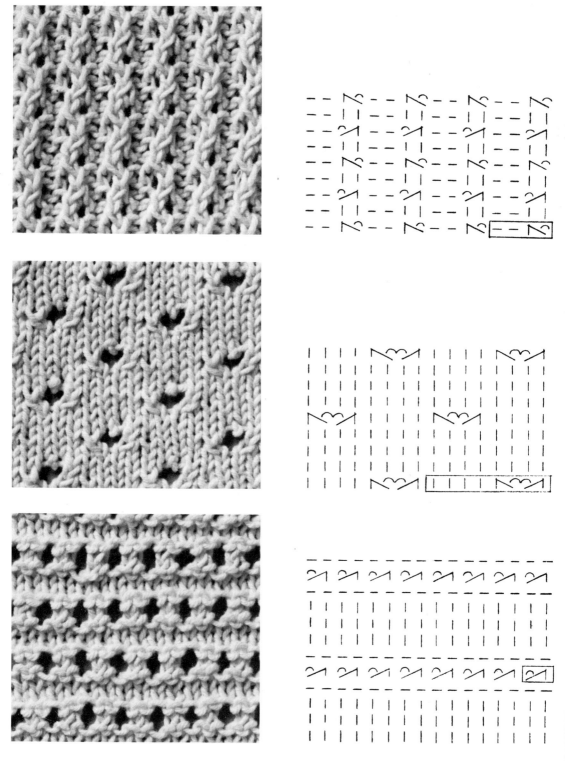

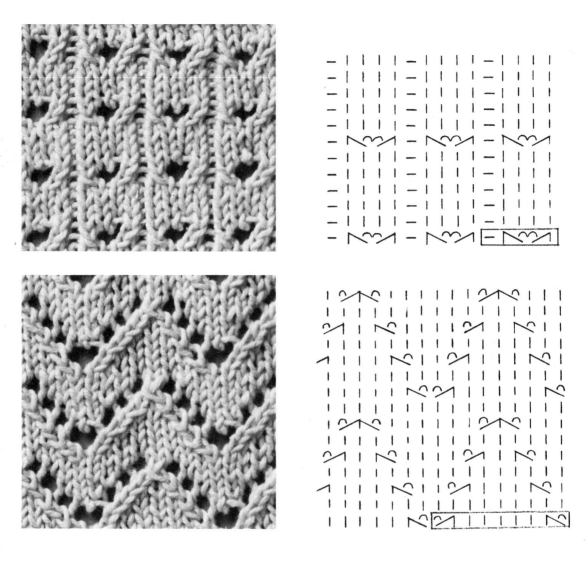

93

Project 21

Baby Bonnet

This bonnet is for infants 1 day to 3 months old. Among the patterns suggested here, the lace patterns would be best for spring while the solid patterns would be warmer for winter.

MATERIAL NEEDED

2 ounces of baby yarn
1 pair of knitting needles, size 2. (See page 8.)
1 yard of silk ribbon or a handmade, twisted tie string. (See page 46.)

WORK METHOD

Casting on
Row knitting
Knotted edge
Star end-decreasing (see photograph)

PATTERN STITCH

Choose from among photographs. Then use the corresponding diagram to figure out how to knit that pattern. (See page 91 for key to symbols.)

Amy M., age 15

KNITTING INSTRUCTIONS

*Knotted edge

1 Cast on number given under photograph.

2 *Rib ½ inch, plain-knit 1, purl 1.

3 *Knit 3½ inches in the pattern stitch. Finish knitting on an inside row.

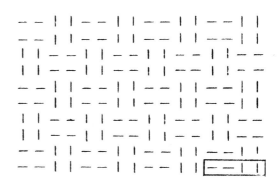

Cast on 84 stitches

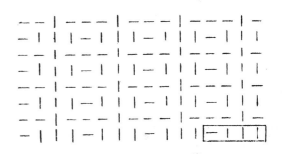

Cast on 83 stitches

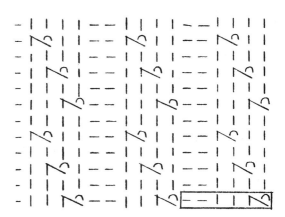

Cast on 84 stitches

95

4 Star end-decrease:
  a *Purl together 2 stitches, plain-knit 8, repeat to end of row. Plain-knit any leftover stitches.
  b *Purl 1 row.
  c *Purl together 2 stitches, plain-knit 7, repeat to end of row. Plain-knit any leftover stitches.
  d *Purl 1 row.
  e *Purl together 2 stitches, plain-knit 6, repeat to end of row. Plain-knit any leftover stitches.
  f *Purl 1 row.

  Continue to decrease as above, plain knitting 5, 4, 3, 2, 1, 0, and plain knitting any leftover stitches.

5 Cut the yarn, leaving 1 arm's length. Using a tapestry needle, draw the yarn through the stitches left on the needle. Remove the needle. Draw the yarn through the stitches again in the same direction and pull the stitches together tightly.

3 Sew the tie strings to the corners. Cut the ends diagonally to prevent fraying.

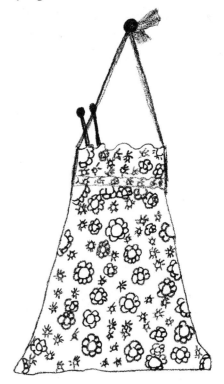

Beatrice R., age 12. Sew a drawstring bag to carry your knitting.

FINISHING INSTRUCTIONS

1 Block by steaming. If knitting needs to be washed, block by patting it into shape when wet on a flat surface and allow to dry.

2 Fold bonnet in half and sew the rounded edge together.

96

Project 22

Baby Sweater: 1 to 8 Months

This little sweater is knitted all in one piece. You knit from side to side instead of the usual bottom to top. It can be worn with the opening at the front or the back.

MATERIAL NEEDED

3 ounces of baby wool or cotton yarn

1 pair of knitting needles, size 2. (See page 8.)
1 stitch holder 4 inches long
1 yard of silk ribbon or a handmade, twisted tie string. (See page 46.)
1 tapestry needle

WORK METHOD

Casting on
Row knitting
Knotted edge
Casting *in* stitches
Binding off
Beading (See page 102.)

Knitted by Ritchie P., age 13

PATTERN STITCH

Choose from among photographs. Then use the corresponding diagram to figure out how to knit that pattern. (See page 91 for key to symbols.)

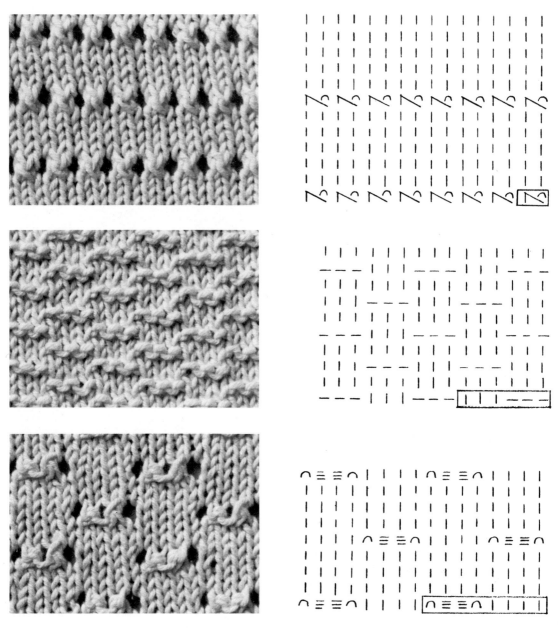

KNITTING INSTRUCTIONS

*Knotted edge

First Half of Front

1 Cast on 70 stitches.

2 *Plain-knit until you have 4 garter rows (border).

3 *(Outside row)   Knit 52 stitches in your pattern stitch or until there are 17 stitches on the needle. These will be knitted in garter rows to form the collar. See photograph.

4 Collar: plain-knit together 2 stitches. Turn the knitting around to the inside row and yarn-over once on the inside with the right-hand needle. Plain-knit 1 stitch. See drawing. Finish the row (53 stitches) in your pattern stitch.

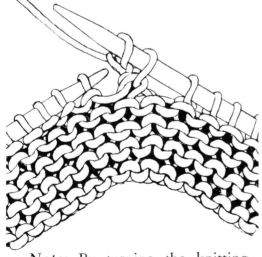

Note: By turning the knitting around you skipped knitting the 17 stitches for the collar.

5 *(Outside row)   Knit in your pattern stitch to 1 stitch before the yarn-over you made in the last row.

6 Collar: plain-knit 1 stitch. Plain-knit the yarn-over but keep it on the left-hand needle. See illustration 1. Plain-knit together the same yarn-over and the next stitch. See illustration 2. Plain-knit to end of row.

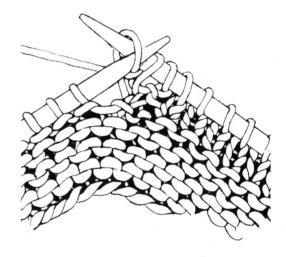

7 *(Inside row)   Plain-knit the 17 collar stitches. Finish the row in your pattern stitch.

8 *(Outside row)   Knit in your pattern stitch until there are 17 stitches left for the collar. Plain-knit the collar stitches.

9 *(Inside row)   Plain-knit the 17 collar stitches. Finish the row in your pattern stitch.

Note: You should now have a small hole at the beginning of the collar and 2 garter rows knitted beyond it. Compare your knitting with the photograph. At this point it is necessary to turn the knitting. The small hole and others to come will be used as markers.

10 Repeat steps 3–9 until the knitting measures 5½ inches. Finish knitting on an inside row.

First Sleeve

1* (Outside row) Knit 41 stitches and put them on a stitch holder. Continue knitting the row.

2 Knit the stitches on the inside row. Cast *in* 41 stitches. Make sure you again have 70 stitches on the needle.

3* Knit about 6 inches for the sleeve. Finish knitting on an inside row.

Compare the pattern stitch on the sleeve with that of the front where you are holding the stitches. The front must have 1 extra row.

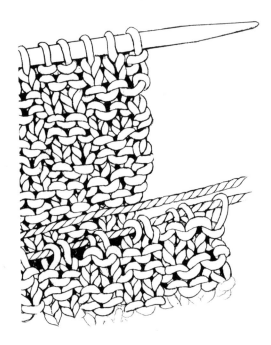

4* (Outside row) Bind off 41 stitches. Continue knitting the row.

5* (Inside row)   Knit the stitches on the needle. Put the stitches that are on the stitch holder onto the empty needle. See illustration. Finish row.

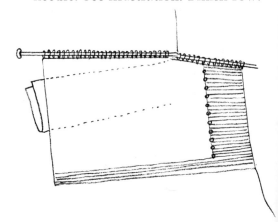

Back

*Knit 8 inches for the back. Finish knitting on an inside row.

Second Sleeve

Knit the same as the first sleeve.

Second Half of Front

1 *Knit 5 ½ inches, ending with a border of garter rows.
2 *Bind off. Do not cut the yarn. Leave the last stitch on the needle.

Completing Collar

1 Pick up and knit a plain stitch between each 2 garter rows along the edge on the outside of the collar. See photograph. Do this by inserting the tip of the needle, front to back, between the first 2 garter rows. Then wrap the yarn around the tip and bring the yarn through to the front.

2 *Plain-knit 1 row.

3 *Knit 1 row of beading: plain-knit together 2 stitches, yarn-over. Repeat to end of row.
4 *Plain-knit 1 row.
5 *Bind off. Cut the yarn leaving 3 inches.

Completing Sleeves

1 Make a slipknot and put it on the needle. Pick up and knit 36–40 (even number) plain stitches along the edge of the sleeve.
2 *Rib 2 ½ inches: plain-knit 1, purl 1.
3 *Bind off in the ribbing pattern. Leave 1 arm's length of yarn for sewing the sleeve together.

FINISHING INSTRUCTIONS

1 Block. (See page 65.)
2 Sew the sleeves together on the inside with overcasting stitches.
3 Sew in all yarn ends.
4 Weave in ribbon. Cut ribbon at a 45-degree angle to keep the fabric from fraying.

Picking up Stitches

By "picking up stitches" along an edge you can add new knitting to finished work. The picked-up stitches are put onto a needle and knitted as usual. The process is often used to add borders around the neck, waist, wrist or ankle. You can also pick up stitches to lengthen the sleeves and waist of a sweater you have outgrown.

KNITTING INSTRUCTIONS

Insert the tip of the needle, front to back, through the top edge of the knitting. Then wrap the yarn around the tip and bring the yarn through to the front (similar to crocheting).

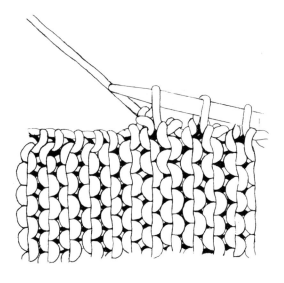

Beading

Beading means to knit a row of holes. It is usually done so you can thread a tie string through the holes.

IN GARTER ROWS AND STOCKINETTE

1 Yarn-over, plain-knit together 2 stitches. Repeat to end of row or round.

2 Next row or round: knit each yarn-over into a regular stitch.

WITHIN THE RIBBING PATTERN: PLAIN 1, PURL 1

1 Yarn-over before the purl stitch, then plain-knit together the plain and purl stitches. Repeat to end of row or round.

2 a Row knitting: next row knit all yarn-overs into plain stitches, purling in between.

b Round knitting: in the next round knit all yarn-overs into purl stitches, plain-knitting in between.

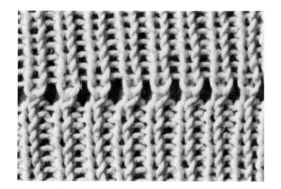

WITHIN THE RIBBING PATTERN: PLAIN 2, PURL 2

1 Slip the second plain stitch, purl 1, then bring the slip stitch over the purl stitch, yarn-over twice. Plain-knit together the second purl stitch and the first plain stitch. Repeat to end of row or round.

2 Next row or round: purl the first yarn-over and plain-knit the second one, otherwise follow your ribbing pattern.

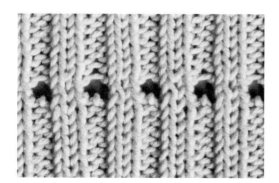

Project 23

Mittens for an Infant

These mittens will nicely fit an infant up to 3 months. They do not need thumbs because babies keep their hands in a fist.

Alexandra D., age 15

MATERIAL NEEDED

2 ounces of baby wool
1 set of 4 short double-pointed knitting needles, size 2. (See page 8.)
1 yard of silk ribbon or a handmade twisted tie string. (See page 46.)
1 tapestry needle

WORK METHOD

Casting on stitches for round knitting. (See page 106.)
Round knitting
Beading
Ending off with 3 stitches between decreasing. (See page 106.)

PATTERN STITCH

Ribbing
Stockinette

KNITTING INSTRUCTIONS
These are for 1 mitten. Knit 2.

1 Cast on 40 stitches, 14 on each of 2 needles, and 12 on a third needle.

2 Rib 1½ inches: plain-knit 1, purl 1.

3 Knit 1 round of beading: yarn-over, slip the plain stitch, purl 1, then pull the slip stitch over the purl stitch and let it go. Repeat to end of round.

4 Plain-knit 1 round. You should still have 14 stitches on each of the first 2 needles and 12 on the third.

5 Plain-knit 2 inches.

6 End off with 3 stitches between decreasing:

Note: Instead of purl decreasing as instructed, you can slip decrease, which blends better into the stockinette background. See illustration page 83.

a Rearrange the stitches on the needles to 15/10/15.

b Purl together 2 stitches, plain-knit 3, repeat to end of round

c Plain-knit 3 rounds.

d Purl together 2 stitches, plain-knit 2, repeat to end of round.

e Plain-knit 2 rounds.

f Purl together 2 stitches, plain-knit 1, repeat to end of round.

g Plain-knit 1 round.

h Purl together 2 stitches, knit 0, repeat to end of round.

7 Cut the yarn, leaving about 8 inches. Using a tapestry needle, draw the yarn through the stitches. Remove the knitting needles. Draw the yarn through the stitches again in the same direction and pull them together tightly.

FINISHING INSTRUCTIONS

1 Bring the yarn to the inside of the knitting and sew it in.

2 Pull the casting-on yarn through the tiny knot, then sew it in on the inside.

3 Weave the tie string through the beading. Cut the ends of silk ribbon diagonally to prevent fraying.

Round Knitting

For round knitting (knitting in circles instead of back and forth in rows), you use a set of 4 or 5 double-pointed needles. You cast on stitches onto all the needles except the one you will knit with. If the knitting is unusually wide you should cast onto more than 4 needles in order not to have more than 20 stitches on a needle.

In round knitting you are always knitting on the outside. *Each round starts at the piece of yarn leftover from casting on (See illustration). The round is completed when you have knitted around to that same point.* You just keep knitting around and around, and the knitting grows longer.

Because there are no "sides" to round knitting, there is no knotted edge to think about. All stitches are knitted.

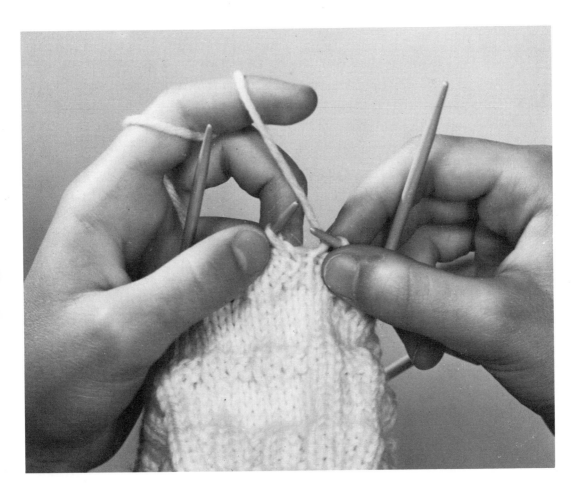

Casting-on Stitches onto 3 Needles

1 Measure out enough yarn for casting on.

2 Cast on 1/3 of the stitches onto the first needle. Slide the stitches to the middle of the needle and let it dangle.

3 Cast on the second 1/3 of the stitches onto the second needle. Make sure there is no gap between stitches from one needle to the next. See illustration. Slide the stitches to the middle of the needle and let it dangle.

4 Cast on the rest of the stitches onto the third needle. Slide them to the middle of the needle.

5 Form a triangle with the needles. See illustration. Slide the stitches on the first needle toward the point and knit them off onto the empty needle.

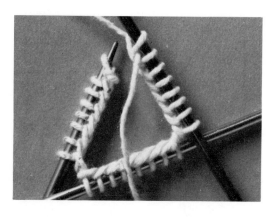

Ending Off in Round Knitting

To make a rounded ending like that on a sock, mitten or hat, you decrease *1 stitch* at a time at regular intervals for an entire round. (Choose decreasing method from page 83.) Decreasing rounds are alternated with a certain number of regular rounds until the knitting comes to an end.

When you are ready to end off the knitting, you must know how many regular stitches to knit between decreasing stitches. Most of the time the instructions will tell you. But if you designed your own project, you would have to figure it out this way: Divide the stitches on the round by 10 and subtract 1. (If 10 doesn't fit exactly, use the nearest number that 10 does divide into.)

Stitches on round	Formula	Stitches between decreasing
72	$70 \div 10 - 1 =$	6
36	$40 \div 10 - 1 =$	3

Start the decreasing round by purling together 2 stitches. Plain-knit the number of in-between stitches you figured out by the above formula. Alternate decreasing and plain stitches to end of round. Then knit the same number of regular rounds as the number of stitches between decreasing stitches. In each succeeding decreasing round the number of stitches between decreasing stitches is reduced by 1, and so is the number of regular rounds knitted on top.

Note: Instead of purling together you can plain-knit together 2 stitches or slip decrease (see page 83.)

If there are 6 stitches between decreasing, follow steps 1 through 8

1 Purl together 2 stitches, plain-knit 6, repeat to end of round.
Plain-knit any leftover stitches.
Plain-knit 6 rounds.

If there are 5 stitches between decreasing, follow steps 2–8

2 Purl together 2 stitches, plain-knit 5, repeat to end of round. Plain-knit 5 rounds.

If there are 4 stitches between decreasing, follow steps 3–8

3 Purl together 2 stitches, plain-knit 4, repeat to end of round.
Plain-knit 4 rounds.

If there are 3 stitches between decreasing, follow steps 4–8

4 Purl together 2 stitches, plain-knit 3, repeat to end of round.
Plain-knit 3 rounds.

If there are 2 stitches between decreasing, follow steps 5–8

5 Purl together 2 stitches, plain-knit 2, repeat to end of round.
plain-knit 2 rounds.

If there is 1 stitch between decreasing, follow steps 6–8

6 Purl together 2 stitches, plain-knit 1, repeat to end of round.
Plain-knit 1 round.

If there are 0 stitches between decreasing, follow steps 7 and 8.

7 Purl together 2 stitches, repeat to end of round.

8 Cut the yarn at 1 arm's length. Thread it through a tapestry needle. String the remaining stitches onto the yarn and draw them together tightly.

Pamela M., age 13

Ski Mittens

Mittens keep your hands warmer than gloves. They are also easier to knit. For skiing, sew suede to the palms and on the inside of the thumbs. The knitting instructions below are for a mitten to fit a 12-year-old. For a different size, trace around the hand. Then knit a gauge and see how many stitches you need to fit across the palm. Double this and add 4 stitches for the thickness of the hand. This will give you the number of stitches to cast on.

MATERIAL NEEDED

4 ounces of knitting worsted
1 set of 4 short, double-pointed knitting needles, size 4. (See page 8.)
1 tapestry needle

WORK METHOD

Casting on
Round knitting
Increasing stitches from yarn-overs
Ending off with 3 stitches between decreasing.

PATTERN STITCH

Ribbing
Stockinette

Knitted by Margot O., age 12

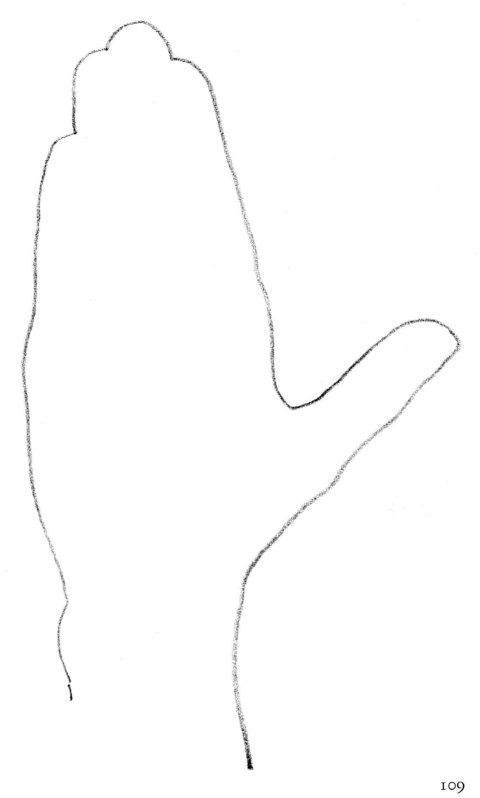

109

KNITTING INSTRUCTIONS

These instructions are for 1 mitten; knit 2 (left and right are the same). They fit the traced hand of a 12-year-old. (See page 109.)

1 Cast on 36 stitches, 12/12/12.

2 Rib about 3 inches for the cuff: plain-knit 2, purl 2.

3 Plain-knit 4 rounds.

4 Place a marker at the beginning of the round. At this point start to increase stitches for the thumb as follows:

    a Yarn-over onto the empty needle, plain-knit the first 2 stitches on the round, yarn-over, then plain-knit the rest of the round.

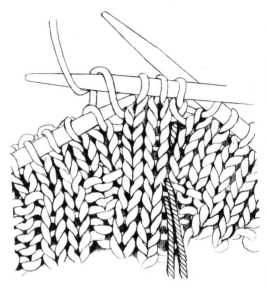

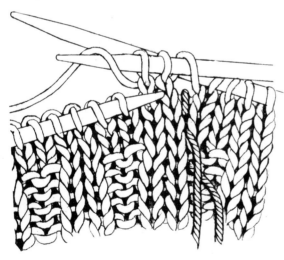

    b Plain-knit 2 rounds. In the first of the 2 rounds knit through the back to each of the 2 yarn-overs. This twists the stitches and avoids a hole.

    c Yarn-over onto the empty needle, plain-knit 4, yarn-over, then plain-knit the rest of the round.

    d Plain-knit 2 rounds.

    e Yarn-over onto the empty needle, plain-knit 6, yarn-over, then plain-knit the rest of the round.

    f Plain-knit 2 rounds.

    g Yarn-over onto the empty needle, plain-knit 8, yarn-over, then plain-knit the rest of the round.

    h Plain-knit 2 rounds.

    i Yarn-over onto the empty needle, plain-knit 10, yarn-over, then plain-knit the rest of the round.

    j Plain-knit 2 rounds.

    k String the first 12 stitches of the round onto a piece of different colored yarn and keep them aside for knitting the thumb later.

There should be 10 stitches left on the needle.

5 Cast *in* 2 stitches onto the empty needle. Plain-knit 1 round. You should now have 12 stitches on each needle.

6 Plain-knit about 3 inches or as many rounds as needed to cover the tip of the little finger.

7 Rearrange the stitches on the needle to 10/15/11. End off with 3 stitches between decreasing. (See page 106.)

COMPLETING THE THUMB

1 Transfer the stitches you are holding on the yarn onto 3 needles, 4/4/4.

2 With the third needle pick up 2 stitches to bridge the gap at the base of the thumb. See illustration. You should now have 14 stitches for knitting the thumb.

3 Plain-knit as many rounds as needed to cover the thumb.

4 Rearrange the stitches to 3/6/5. End off the thumb with 1 stitch between decreasing.

5 Cut the yarn, leaving 4 inches. Using a tapestry needle draw the yarn through the stitches. Remove the knitting needles. Draw the yarn through again in the same direction and pull the stitches together tightly.

FINISHING INSTRUCTIONS

1 Sew in yarn ends. (See page 140.)

2 Sew a few stitches over the gap at the base of the thumb if needed.

Knitted by Julia M., age 13

Project 25

Dolls

Baby-Yarn Doll

*These dolls are about 12 inches tall.
You can knit pullovers, socks, scarves
and hats for them by following the instructions in this book. Knit a gauge
and fit it on the body of the doll for
the number of stitches to cast on.*

MATERIAL NEEDED

2 ounces of cotton yarn, baby yarn, or
sport yarn
1 set of short double-pointed needles,
size 2. (See page 8.)
Stuffing material. (See page 54.)
1 tapestry needle

WORK METHOD

Casting on
Round knitting
Row knitting
Knotted edge
Casting *in* stitches
Ending off with 2 stitches between de-
creasing
Binding off

PATTERN STITCH

Ribbing
Stockinette

KNITTING INSTRUCTIONS
*Knotted edge

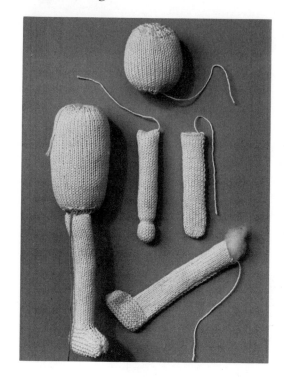

Head

1 Cast on 40 stitches, 12/12/16.

2 Rib 3 rounds (bottom edge):
   plain-knit 1, purl 1.

3 Plain-knit 24 rounds.

4 End off with 2 stitches between decreasing. (See page 106.)

Body

1 Cast on 40 stitches, 12/12/16.

2 Rib 3 rounds (top edge): plain-
   knit 1, purl 1.

3 Plain-knit 40 rounds.

4 End off with 2 stitches between decreasing.

Small doll knitted by Katherine M., age 12

Arms

1 Cast on 15 stitches, 6/6/3.

2 Plain-knit 40 rounds.

3 End off with 1 stitch between decreasing.

Legs

Row knitting. Use the same two needles throughout.

1 Cast on 18 stitches.

2* Stockinette 49 rows. Finish knitting on an inside row.

3* Plain-knit 9 stitches, cast in 6 stitches onto the right-hand needle (for the foot), hold the rest of the stitches on the left-hand needle without knitting them.

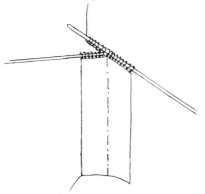

4* Plain-knit 8 garter rows on the needle that has 15 stitches.

5* Bind off the 15 stitches.

6 Cast on 6 stitches onto the empty needle, then plain-knit the 9 stitches you have been holding.

7* Plain-knit 8 garter rows.

8* Bind off. Leave 1 arm's length of yarn for sewing.

FINISHING INSTRUCTIONS

Head and Body

1 Stuff the head firmly.

2 Thread the yarn leftover from casting on, into a tapestry needle. Weave the yarn through the loops around the open edge. See illustration. Pull the opening together tightly and fasten it with 2 tiny stitches across the hole.

3 Sew in all yarn ends.

4 Stuff the body to your liking. Close up the same way as the head (step 2).

Arms

1 Stuff.

2 Sew the opening together.

3 Wind a piece of yarn twice around the wrist tightly. Make a knot and sew the ends into the arm.

Legs

1 Sew foot together.

2 Stuff.

3 Sew up leg and stuff.

Joints

1 Sew head and arms to the body.

2 Sew the legs to the body while the doll is in a sitting position.

Hair

1 Choose yarn of the hair color you want and cut about 80 strands that are double the hair-length desired.

2 Fold each strand in half and loop it through the top of the head the way you attach fringe (see page 44). Or, instead of fringe, you can glue a piece of fur to the head.

Face—see photograph

If you like to imagine a face showing different moods, embroider eyes only. If the doll is for a very young child, it is better to show all features: eyes, nose, and mouth.

Thick-Yarn Doll

Sasha C., age 12

MATERIAL NEEDED

2 ounces of knitting worsted
1 set of 4 double-pointed knitting needles, size 4. (See page 7.)
Stuffing material (See page 54.)
1 tapestry needle

WORK METHOD AND PATTERN STITCH

See baby-yarn doll.

KNITTING INSTRUCTIONS

*Knotted edge

Head

1 Cast on 36 stitches, 12/12/12.

2 Rib 3 rounds (bottom edge): plain-knit 1, purl 1.

3 Plain—knit 17 rounds.

4 End off with 2 stitches between decreasing. (See page 106.)

Body

1 Cast on 36 stitches, 12/12/12.

2 Rib 3 rounds, plain-knit 1, purl 1.

3 Plain-knit 28 rounds.

4 End off with 2 stitches between decreasing.

Arms

Row knitting

1 Cast on 12 stitches.

2*Stockinette 31 rows.

3 Plain-knit together 2 stitches for the entire row. Cut the yarn leaving 8 inches. Using a tapestry needle draw the yarn through the stitches. See illustration. Remove the knitting needle and pull the stitches together tightly.

Legs

Row knitting. Use the same two needles throughout.

1 Cast on 14 stitches.

2*Stockinette 33 rows. Finish knitting on an inside row.

3*Plain-knit 6 stitches. Cast *in* 5 stitches onto the right-hand needle (for the foot), hold the rest of the stitches on the left-hand needle without knitting them.

4*Plain-knit 5 garter rows on the needle that has 12 stitches.

5*Bind off the 12 stitches.

6 Cast on 5 stitches onto the empty needle, then plain-knit the 7 stitches you have been holding.

7*Plain-knit 5 garter rows.

8*Bind off. Leave 1 arm's length of yarn for sewing.

FINISHING INSTRUCTIONS

Same as baby-yarn doll. (See page 114.)

Heavily Textured Patterns for Row Knitting

The following patterns cannot be indicated on diagrams. To try out the patterns, cast on 16 stitches. Make sure you knit each pattern row on the side of the work indicated. You may want to vary the patterns by knitting rows of stockinette between patterns.

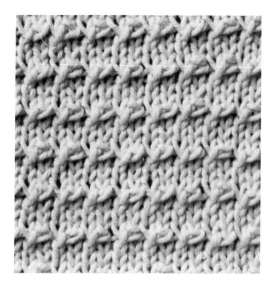

*Knotted edge

PATTERN A

Cast on an even number of stitches.

First row (outside): *plain-knit all stitches.

Second row (inside): *yarn-over, plain-knit 2, then bring the yarn-over over the 2 knitted stitches and slide it off the needle. Repeat this sequence to end of row.

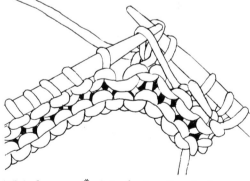

Third row: *plain-knit all stitches.
Fourth row: *purl all stitches.
Repeat rows 1–4.

Knitted by Nancy H., age 14

PATTERN B

(This pattern has a tendency to stretch horizontally, so be careful in gauging your work. The knitting looks the same on both sides, making it ideal for a wraparound scarf. It is also ideal for a warm, bulky ski sweater.)

Cast on an even number of stitches.
First row (inside): *plain-knit 1 stitch, then bring the yarn in front of the left-hand needle and slip the yarn and the next stitch as if to purl, over onto the right-hand needle.
Repeat this sequence to end of row.

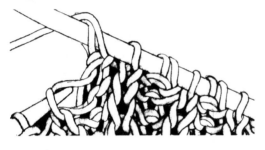

Second row (outside): *plain-knit together the yarn-over and the slipped stitch, then bring yarn in front of the left-hand needle and slip the yarn and the next stitch as if to purl, over onto the right-hand needle. Repeat this sequence to end of row.

Repeat the second row for all following rows.

Note: The pattern will not begin to appear until you have knitted several rows.

PATTERN C

Cast on an even number of stitches.
First row (outside): *plain-knit all stitches.
Second row (inside): *plain-knit 1 stitch, then bring the yarn in front of

the left-hand needle and slip the next stitch as if to purl, dropping the yarn across the front of the stitch. Repeat this sequence to end of row.

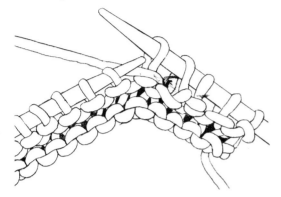

Repeat rows 1 and 2.

PATTERN D
(This kind of knitting is called Tunisian Stitch; it is very solid and heavy. The structure of the knitted stitches lends itself to cross-stitch embroidery. (See page 144).

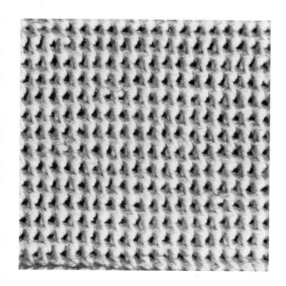

Cast on any number of stitches.

First row (inside): *Bring the yarn in front of the left-hand needle and slip the yarn and the next stitch as if to purl over onto the right-hand needle. Again bring the yarn in front of the left-hand needle and slip it together with the next stitch as if to purl over onto the right-hand needle.

Repeat to end of row.

Second row (outside): *plain-knit together the yarn over and the slipped stitch *through the back;* this will give it a twist. Repeat to end of row.

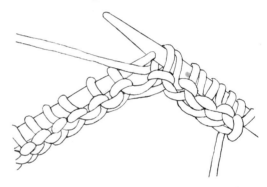

Repeat rows 1 and 2.

Serena R., age 12

How to Design and Knit Cable Patterns

Cable patterns have a ropelike appearance with 2 "strands" intertwining usually against a plain background. You have probably seen cabling on tennis and ski sweaters and sport socks.

DESIGNING CABLE PATTERNS

Your cable design may form a sort of ribbing pattern or the cabling may be treated as a dominant feature against a plain background of stockinette or purl stitches. To make your design you must decide on:

1 how many cables to have and how far apart they should be;

2 how wide each cable should be (generally, unless it is a special kind of cable, the width should never be more than 12 stitches and must always be an even number of stitches);

3 how many purl stitches to have bordering the cable;

4 how many straight rows to knit over each cable row (the row where you cross the strands). There should be at least as many rows knitted over the crossing or cable row as the number of stitches the cable is wide. The number of straight rows between cabling must always be uneven because you cable only on the outside rows.

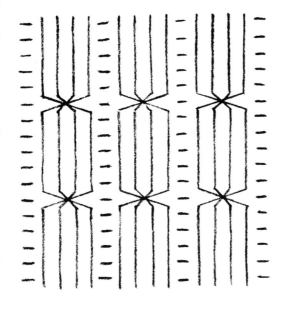

KNITTING INSTRUCTIONS

Outside Row

1 Knit to the stitches you want to cable.

2 Put the first half of the stitches to be cabled onto an extra, double-pointed needle or wooden match. Plain-knit the second half of the stitches.

3 Take the cable needle, in your left hand and plain-knit the stitches on the needle.

4 Resume regular knitting, cabling with the extra needle where planned.

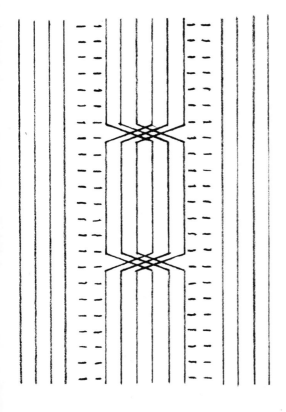

Inside Row

Purl over all purl stitches and plain-knit over all plain stitches.

Project 26

Baby Pullover: 8 to 12 Months

This raglan-sleeve pullover knits quite quickly. You may want to make several of them in different colors, yarn textures and pattern stitches. It fits loosely and it will take a long time for a child to grow out of it.

Knitted for her niece by Alexandra D., age 15

MATERIAL NEEDED

4 ounces of sport yarn
1 pair of short knitting needles, size 2
A drawstring made of yarn

WORK METHOD

Casting on
Row knitting
Knotted edge
Decreasing by knitting together stitches
Beading (See page 102.)
Binding off

PATTERN STITCH

Garter rows, or choose your own

KNITTING INSTRUCTIONS

The pullover is knitted in 4 parts: back, front and two sleeves. You may want to knit all ribbing on smaller needles for a tighter fit. (See page 75.)

*Knotted edge

Back

1 Cast on 82 stitches.

2 *Rib 1¼ inches: plain 1, purl 1.

3 *Knit 6 inches in your pattern stitch.

4 *Decrease for raglan shaping: plain-knit together the last 2 stitches on every row until you have 58 stitches left on the needle.

5 *Plain-knit 1 row.

6 *Rib 2½ inches: start ribbing with a purl stitch. Finish on an inside row.

7 *Knit 1 row of beading: plain-knit together 2 stitches, yarn-over. Repeat.

8 *Purl 1 row.

9 *Bind off. Leave 1 arm's length of yarn for sewing.

Front

Knit the same as back.

Sleeve

1 Cast on 54 stitches.

2 *Rib 2½ inches: plain 1, purl 1.

3 *Knit 6 inches of your pattern stitch.

4 *Decrease for raglan shaping: plain-knit together the last 2 stitches on every row until you have 30 stitches left on the needle.

5 *Plain-knit 1 row.

6 *Rib, matching the front and back of the pullover. Start ribbing with a purl stitch. Finish on an inside row.

7 *Knit 1 row of beading: plain-knit together 2 stitches, yarn-over. Repeat.

8 *Purl 1 row.

9 *Bind off. Leave 1 arm's length of yarn for sewing.

FINISHING INSTRUCTIONS

1 Sew the pullover together on the inside. Overcast together all ribbing borders. Sew together the rest of the pullover with backstitches alongside the knotted edges.

2 Weave the tie string through the beading.

Beth P., age 11

123

Knitted by Sita S., age 17

Raglan Sleeve Pullover

This pullover can be knitted to any size and will look well on a boy or girl, man or woman. It has a round neck which can become a turtleneck by knitting more ribbing.

MATERIAL NEEDED

Use any kind of yarn you want. Ask store clerk about quantity.

1 pair of knitting needles (Size depends on yarn chosen. See chart on page 7.)

Knitting model (a sweater of the right size).

WORK METHOD

Row knitting

Knotted edge

Decreasing by knitting together stitches

Binding off

PATTERN STITCH

Ribbing

Stockinette, or choose your own pattern stitch

First knit a gauge. See how many times the width of the gauge will fit across the model sweater from armpit to armpit. Multiply the number of stitches in the gauge by the number of times the gauge fits across the model. See drawing. This will give you the number of stitches to cast on for the back or the front (they are the same). Add or subtract a few stitches to adjust to the exact size. Measure with your gauge around the sleeve of the model just above the wrist for the number of stitches to cast on for the sleeve.

KNITTING INSTRUCTIONS

*Knotted edge

This pullover is knitted in 4 separate parts: back, front, and 2 sleeves.

Back

1 Cast on required number of stitches.
2 *Rib border to desired length.
3 *Stockinette or knit your own pattern stitch straight up to the armpit. Compare length with model pullover.
4 *Decrease for raglan shaping: plain-knit together the last 2 stitches on every row. Stop decreasing 1 inch below the neckline of the model or when you have about 30 stitches left. Finish knitting on an inside row.
5 *Plain-knit 1 row.
6 *Rib about ½ inch for a round neck, and about 6 inches if you want to make a turtleneck.
7 *Bind off in the ribbing pattern. Leave 1 arm's length of yarn for sewing.

Front

Knit the same as back.

Sleeve

1 Cast on required number of stitches.

2 *Rib border to the desired length.
3 Increase: plain-knit 2 stitches out of the first and last stitches on the outside row, knitting your pattern in between. (See page 82.)
4 Count the decrease stitches on the back along one side of the raglan shaping. See drawing. Multiply this number by 2 and add 20. This is the total number of stitches the sleeve must be increased to. Half the stitches will be added on each side of the sleeve.

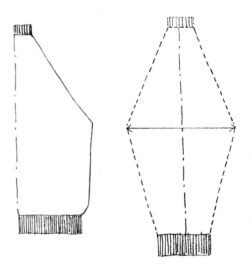

5 Measure the sleeve of the model from above the cuff to the armpit. Space the increasing rows evenly in between.

6* Knit the sleeve to the armpit, adding stitches as instructed in step 3.

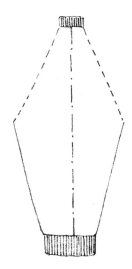

7* Decrease for raglan shaping: plain-knit together the last 2 stitches on every row. Stop decreasing when you have 20 stitches left. Finish on an inside row.

8* Plain-knit 1 row.

9* Rib, matching the front and back.

10* Bind off in the ribbing pattern. Leave 1 arm's length of yarn for sewing.

FINISHING INSTRUCTIONS

Sew the pullover together on the inside. Overcast together all ribbing borders. Sew together the rest of the pullover with backstitches along the knotted edges.

Project 28

Raglan Sleeve Cardigan

The only difference between a raglan sleeve cardigan and a raglan sleeve pullover is the front. The front of a cardigan is divided in half like a jacket. Otherwise the knitting instructions are the same as for a pullover. You use the same materials and work methods for each.

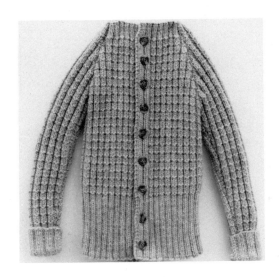

KNITTING INSTRUCTIONS

Back and Sleeves

Follow instructions for raglan sleeve pullover. (See page 126.)

Front, Left Half

Cast on half the number of stitches used for the back, plus 4. The *first* 8 stitches of the first row are the border stitches. Knit these 8 stitches in garter rows or ribbing all the way up. See drawing.

Front, Right Half

Cast on the same number of stitches as you did for the left half. Use the *last* 8 stitches in the first row for the border. Make the first buttonhole when the knitting measures 1 inch. (See page 128 for how to knit a buttonhole.) Start each hole in the center of the border and on an outside row. Bind off from 2 to 4 stitches depending on the size of the button you plan to use. In the following row cast back in as many stitches as you bound off. See drawing. Space the buttonholes about 2 inches apart.

FINISHING INSTRUCTIONS

Lay the border with the buttonholes over the opposite border. Mark with pins through the holes where the buttons go, centered in the border. Sew on the buttons with fine, matching cotton thread. Use the thread doubled. See raglan sleeve pullover for remaining finishing instructions.

How to Make a Buttonhole

To make a buttonhole, 2 rows of knitting are needed. Starting on an outside row, knit to the place where the buttonhole should begin. Bind off as many stitches as you want the buttonhole to be long. Finish the row.

On the next (inside) row knit to the beginning of the buttonhole. Cast back *in* as many stitches as you bound off in the row before.

Project 29

Matchbox Cradle

Eliza B., age 13

While making this little cradle you will also be learning how to knit the heel of a sock.

MATERIAL NEEDED
Leftover baby yarn or sport yarn
1 set of double-pointed knitting needles, size 2
The bottoms of 2 matchboxes, about 1½ inches x 2 inches

WORK METHOD
Round knitting
Row knitting
Decreasing with a slip stitch
Decreasing by purling together stitches
Picking up stitches
Binding off

PATTERN STITCH
Ribbing
Stockinette

KNITTING INSTRUCTIONS

Sides of Cradle

1 Cast on 40 stitches onto 4 needles, 10/10/10/10.

2 Rib 4 rounds: plain 1, purl 1.

3 On the next round continue to rib on the first, second and third needles. Plain-knit all stitches on the fourth needle.

Back of Cradle

1 Set aside the empty needle. With the fourth needle, plain-knit to the last stitch on the first needle; slip the last stitch as if to purl. See illustration. From now on knit only on the needle with the most stitches.

2 Turn the knitting around to the inside (purl stitches). Plain-knit the first 2 stitches, then purl until there are 2 stitches left on the needle. Plain-knit 1 and slip as if to purl the last.

3 Turn the knitting around to the outside (plain stitches). Plain-knit all but the last stitch on the needle; slip as if to purl the last one.

4 Turn the knitting around to the inside. Repeat steps 2 and 3 until the straight-knitted part is about 1 inch long.

5 Look at your knitting. You will see purl stitches forming along each edge. Count these purl stitches on one side. Continue knitting as in steps 2 and 3 until there are 8 purl stitches along each edge. Finish knitting on an inside row.

Top of Cradle

1 Divide the 20 stitches on the needle into 2 equal parts. Mark the center of each half with contrasting-colored yarn.

2 Plain-knit to 1 stitch before the second marker. Slip the stitch before the marker. Plain-knit the stitch right after the marker and pull the slip stitch over the knitted stitch (similar to binding off). Turn the knitting around to the inside (purl stitches).

3 Slip the first stitch as if to purl. Purl to 1 stitch before the marker. Purl together the stitches before and after the marker. Turn the knitting around to the outside (plain stitches).

4 Slip the first stitch. Plain-knit to 1 stitch before the gap that has ap-

peared on the needle. Slip the stitch before the gap. Plain-knit the stitch after the gap and pull the slip stitch over the knitted stitch. Turn to the inside.

5 Slip the first stitch as if to purl. Purl to 1 stitch before the gap. Purl together the stitches before and after the gap. Turn to the outside.

6 Repeat steps 4 and 5 until all stitches to the outside of the gaps have been decreased. Finish knitting on an inside row. Remove the markers.

3 Rib the stitches on the second and third needles onto 2 separate needles.

4 With the empty fifth needle pick up the 8 stitches along the other edge as in step 2. See illustration. Then plain-knit to the end of the round. You should have 13 stitches on the fourth needle.

Roof and Sides of Cradle

1 Plain-knit to the center of the needle and mark the place with a piece of yarn. You will be round knitting again from this point on.

2 Using the empty needle, plain-knit the stitches to the edge of the straight-knitted part. Pick up a stitch from each edge stitch onto the same needle, alongside the straight-knitted part (8 stitches). See illustration. You should now have 13 stitches on the first needle of the round.

5 Bind off all stitches on the next round loosely. Bind off the stitches on the second and third needles in the ribbing pattern.

6 Cut the yarn, leaving about 3 inches.

FINISHING INSTRUCTIONS

1 Sew in yarn ends. (See page 140.)

2 Fit around matchbox bottoms as shown in illustration.

Project 30
Socks

Although the knitting instructions are for plain knitted socks, the steps are the same for fancier ones.

MATERIAL NEEDED

8 ounces of sport yarn (wool mixed with synthetic) for knee socks, a little less for men's socks
1 set of 5 double-pointed knitting needles, size 2

WORK METHOD

Round knitting
Row knitting for the heel
Decreasing with a slip stitch
Decreasing by purling together stitches
Picking up stitches
End-decreasing

PATTERN STITCH

Ribbing
Stockinette

KNITTING INSTRUCTIONS

Knit a gauge on 20 stitches with the wool and needles you are going to use for your socks. You will use the gauge in figuring out the number of stitches to cast on.

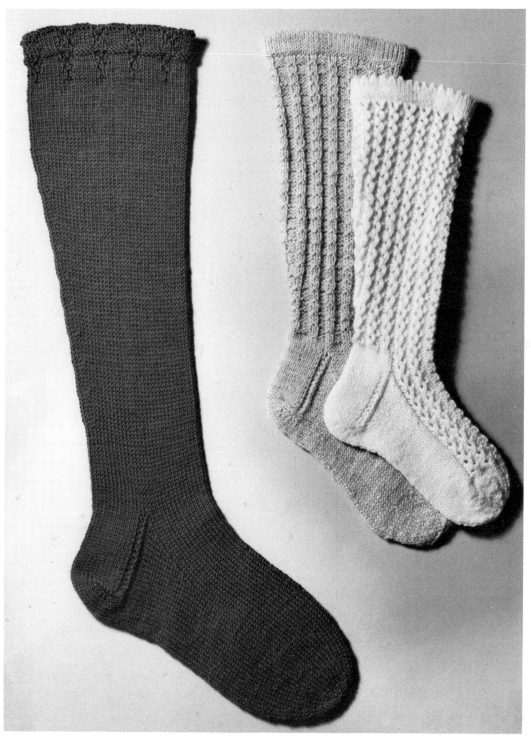

Knitted by Swiss children, 5th grade

Knee Socks

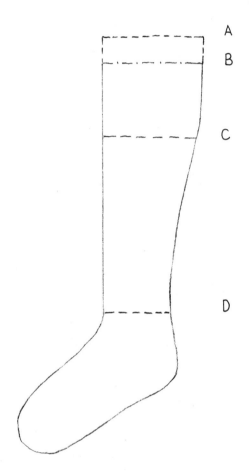

Capital letters, A, B, C, and D refer to drawing.

With a tape measure or strip of paper, measure around the calf of the leg. Use the gauge to find the number of stitches to cast on (the number should divide by 4).

1 Cast on the stitches equally onto 4 needles.

2 Plain-knit 1 inch. (This part will be folded under to hold a garter.)

3 Purl 1 round B

4 Plain-knit 1 inch.

Leg

1 Plain-knit from 1½ to 4 inches. Try on. Knitting should reach to top of calf B–C.

2 From C to D you decrease to follow the shape of the calf. Mark the beginning of the round with a piece of yarn.

   a Plain-knit the first stitch, purl together the second and third stitches, plain-knit to the last 3 stitches on the round, purl together 2 and plain-knit the last stitch. You have decreased 2 stitches.

   b Plain-knit from 8 to 12 rounds (the longer the leg, the more rounds between decreasing).

   c Repeat steps a and b until you have decreased one-quarter of the stitches you had cast on.

   d Divide the stitches evenly among the 4 needles again. Try on the sock. If the knitting does not reach to the heel D, plain-knit to that point.

Straight Part of Heel
(row knitting)

The heel is knitted back and forth with the stitches on the fourth and first needles. Set aside the empty needle.

1 With the fourth needle, plain-knit to the last stitch on the first needle; slip as if to purl the last stitch. See illustration. From now on you knit only on the needle with the most stitches.

2 Turn the knitting around to the inside (purl stitches). Plain-knit the first 2 stitches, then purl until there are 2 stitches left on the needle. Plain-knit 1 and slip as if to purl the last.

3 Turn the knitting around to the outside (plain stitches). Plain-knit all but the last stitch on the needle; slip as if to purl the last one.

4 Turn to the inside. Repeat steps 2 and 3 until the heel is about 1 inch long.

5 Look at your knitting. You will see purl stitches forming along each edge. Count these purl stitches on one side. Continue knitting as in steps 2 and 3 until the number of purl stitches is half the number of stitches on the heel needle *less 2*. Finish knitting on an inside row.

Turning the Heel

1 Divide the stitches on the heel needle in half. Mark the center of each half with contrasting yarn.

2 Plain-knit to 1 stitch before the second marker. Slip the stitch before the marker. Plain-knit the stitch right after the marker and

pull the slip stitch over the knitted stitch (similar to binding off). Turn to the inside.

3 Slip as if to purl the first stitch. Purl to 1 stitch before the marker. Purl together the stitches before and after the marker. Turn to the outside.

4 Slip the first stitch. Plain-knit to 1 stitch before the gap on the needle. Slip the stitch before the gap. Plain-knit the stitch after the gap and pull the slip stitch over the knitted stitch. Turn to the inside.

5 Slip as if to purl the first stitch. Purl to 1 stitch before the gap. Purl together the stitches before and after the gap. Turn to the outside.

6 Repeat steps 4 and 5 until all stitches to the outside of gaps have been decreased. Finish knitting on

an inside row. Remove the markers.

Completing the Heel

1 Plain-knit to the center of the heel needle and mark the place with a piece of yarn. You will be round knitting again from this point on.

2 Using the empty needle, plain-knit the stitches to the edge of the heel. Pick up a stitch from each edge stitch alongside the heel onto the same needle (as many as you have purl stitches along the edge). See illustration.

3 Plain-knit the stitches on the second and third needles onto separate needles.

4 With the fifth needle pick up the same number of stitches along the other edge of the heel as in step 2. See illustration. Then plain-knit to the end of the round.

Instep

1 Plain-knit 2 rounds.

2 Plain-knit to the last 2 stitches on the first needle, purl together these 2 stitches. Plain-knit the stitches on the second and third needles. Purl together the first 2 stitches on the fourth needle. Plain-knit to the end of the round.

3 Repeat steps 1 and 2 until you have the same number of stitches on the round as you did before you started the heel.

Straight Part of Foot

1 Plain-knit until the knitting covers the small toe. Try on the sock occasionally to check length.

2 End-decrease: (follow the rule on page 106).
Allow 2½ inches for 6-stitch end-decreasing.
Allow 2 inches for 5-stitch end-decreasing.
Allow 1½ inches for 4-stitch end-decreasing.
Allow 1 inch for 3-stitch end-decreasing.

Jennifer M., age 10

137

Men's Sock

KNITTING INSTRUCTIONS

Border

1 Cast on required number of stitches. (See page 134.)

2 Knit a 2-inch border, A–B, in ribbing: either plain 1, purl 1; or plain 2, purl 2.

Leg

Knit about 8 inches to bottom of leg, C either in stockinette or in the ribbing used in the border (or another pattern).

Heel, Foot, and Toe

Follow from straight part of heel under instructions for knee socks. (See page 135.)

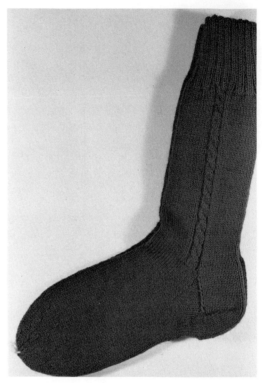

Knitted for her father by Diana H., age 14

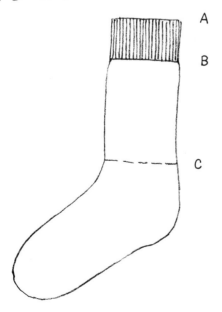

Short Socks

KNITTING INSTRUCTIONS

Border

1. Cast on required number of stitches for leg at height you wish socks to reach. (See page 134.)

2. Knit a border 1 inch long in ribbing: plain 1, purl 1 (A–B).

Leg

Knit 3 or 4 inches to bottom of leg, C in either stockinette, ribbing or another pattern stitch.

Heel, Foot, and Toe

Follow from straight part of heel under instructions for knee socks. (See page 135.)

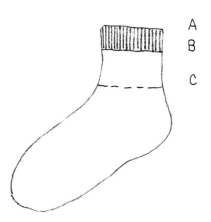

Knitted by Swiss children, 4th and 6th grades

Sewing Instructions for Finishing Knitting

How to Sew in Yarn Ends

All yarn ends must be ended off properly. *Never* just cut them off. Choose from the following the way that is best for your project:

1 Sew yarn ends through the knotted edge for about 1 ½ inches.

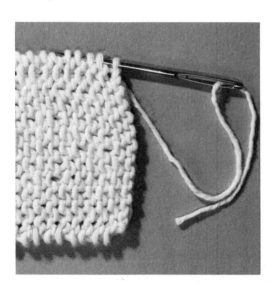

2 Sew yarn ends through knitting of the same color on the inside for about the length of the tapestry needle.

3 Undo the knot on the inside. Cross the 2 yarn ends and sew them through knitting of the same color in opposite directions. Sew through stitches for about the length of the tapestry needle.

4 At the tip of a mitten or sock, or in the ribbing pattern, sew in yarn ends in the shape of the letter U. Leave a small loop at the curve to allow for stretching.

How to Sew a Seam

You make a seam when you fold knitting in half and sew 2 edges together. You also make a seam when you sew together 2 separate knitted parts.

SEWING TOGETHER THE CASTING-ON EDGE

Sew the first stitch through the small knot that you will find in the corner opposite the piece of yarn leftover from casting on. Then overcast to-

gether, the casting-on loops as shown in the illustration. Be careful not to skip a loop.

SEWING TOGETHER THE BINDING-OFF EDGE

Overcast together the *outside half* of each chain stitch as illustrated. Be careful not to skip a chain stitch.

SEWING TOGETHER THE KNOTTED EDGE

Sew the first stitch through the small knot that you will find in the corner opposite the piece of yarn leftover from casting on. Then overcast both sides by sewing through the knots at the end of each garter row. Be careful not to skip a row.

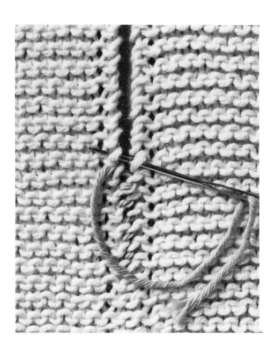

SEWING A SEAM IN THE STOCKINETTE AND OTHER PATTERNS

Turn the knitting inside out. Pin together the edges. With backstitches sew alongside the knotted edge. (For backstitch see page 144.) *Exception:* When the knitting is very narrow,

like the arms and legs for a doll, it is difficult to turn it inside out after sewing. Therefore, overcast together the knotted edges on the *outside*. See sewing together borders above.

SEWING TOGETHER BORDERS

Borders are usually knitted in the ribbing pattern. Sew them together through the knots alongside the edges as shown in the illustration. This makes the seam look the same on each side, which is important if you plan to fold over the ribbing. Be careful on which side you sew in the yarn ends, so they will not show on the outside of the turned-up ribbing.

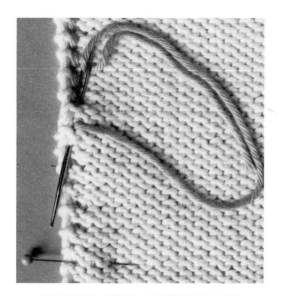

SEWING THE CASTING-ON
EDGE TO THE
BINDING-OFF EDGE

Thread the yarn end left for sewing. Sew the first stitch through the loop made by the last stitch you casted on. See illustration. Pick up the outside half of the chain stitches and the casting-on loops on the other side. Be careful not to miss a stitch on either side.

How to Sew Together
Stuffed Parts

Pin the 2 parts together where you want to attach them. Then sew them together with small running stitches, sewing 1 stitch in one part, the next stitch in the other part.

Sewing Stitches
You Need
to Know

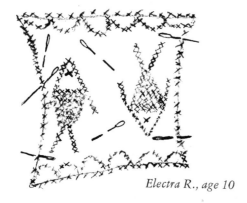

Electra R., age 10

1 Running Stitch

Worked from right to left.

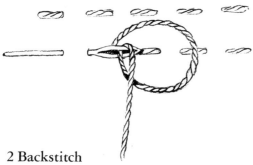

2 Backstitch

Worked from right to left.

3 Cross Stitch

Worked from right to left.

   a Make first diagonal stitch from A to C.

   b Make second diagonal stitch from D to B.

Note: The second diagonal stitch must always cross the first, facing in the same direction.

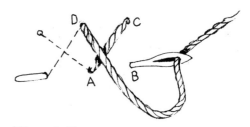

4 French Knot

Used wherever needed.

5 Duplicating Stitch

   a Horizontally: work from right to left.

   b Vertically: work from bottom to top.

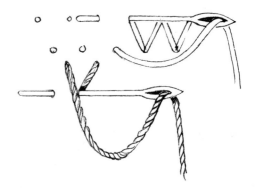

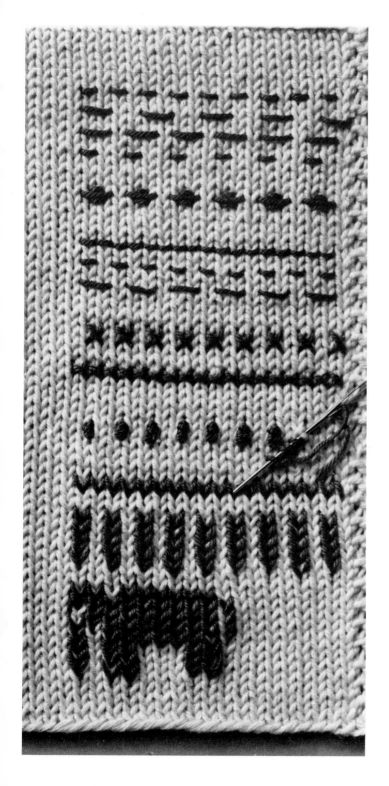

Running stitch

Backstitch

Cross Stitch

French Knot

Duplicating stitch

Index